GEORGE ARMSTRONG CUSTER

SOUTH
DAKOTA
BIOGRAPHY
SERIES

GEORGE ARMSTRONG CUSTER

A MILITARY LIFE

SANDY BARNARD

South Dakota
Historical Society
Press *Pierre*

George Armstrong Custer is Volume 7 in the South Dakota Biography Series.

 This publication is funded, in part, by the Deadwood
Publications Fund provided by the City of Deadwood and
the Deadwood Historic Preservation Commission.

Library of Congress Cataloging-in-Publication data
Names: Barnard, Sandy, author.
Title: George Armstrong Custer : a military life / Sandy Barnard.
Description: Pierre : South Dakota Historical Society Press, [2021] |
Series: South Dakota biography series | Includes bibliographical
references and index. | Summary: "George Armstrong Custer notoriously
died at the hands of Lakota and Northern Cheyenne forces at the Battle
of the Little Bighorn in June 1876. Yet, in addition to his fights against
Plains Indian people, Custer also fought in the Civil War, led troops during
Reconstruction in the Southern states, and explored the Black Hills for the
federal government. Sandy Barnard's new biography, George Armstrong
Custer: A Military Life, explores Custer's life and highlights the complex
nature of his experiences and legacy"—Provided by publisher.
Identifiers: LCCN 2021000515 | ISBN 9781941813232 (paperback)
Subjects: LCSH: Custer, George A. (George Armstrong), 1839–1876. |
Custer, George A. (George Armstrong), 1839–1876—Influence. |
Generals—United States—Biography. | United States. Army—Biography. |
United States—History—Civil War, 1861–1865—Biography. | Indians of
North America—Wars—West (U.S.)
Classification: LCC E467.1.C99 B244 2021 | DDC 973.8/2092 [B]—dc23
LC record available at https://lccn.loc.gov/2021000515

Printed in the United States of America

The paper in this book meets the guidelines for permanence and
durability of the Committee on Production Guidelines for Book Longevity
of the Council on Library Resources.

Please visit our website at sdhspress.com

25 24 23 22 21   1 2 3 4 5

Cover and frontispiece: George Armstrong Custer in 1865. Photograph by
Mathew B. Brady Studio. *Library of Congress*

Designed and set in Arnhem type by Rich Hendel

To Betty Barnard,
my wife, best friend, and
"historical assistant" for
some fifty-five years.

Contents

Acknowledgments

Throughout my years as a researcher and writer studying the United States Civil War and postbellum Indian wars, I have been assisted by countless people who were willing to provide guidance and support. It has certainly been true with this project about the life and career of Lieutenant Colonel George Armstrong Custer.

As a youngster in the 1950s, I probably developed my interest in Custer through the 1956 novel, *The Great Scoop* by Loring MacKaye and the 1957 Walt Disney movie, *Tonka*. Both offered highly fictionalized treatments of the story of the Battle of the Little Big Horn, but each in its own way was fun to read or to watch back then. A central historical character in them was newspaper reporter Mark H. Kellogg of the *Bismarck (D.T.) Tribune*, but I do not recall paying much attention to him in those mid-1950s.

Fast forward to 29 July 1980. I was now a journalism professor at Indiana State University when I made my first visit to Custer (now Little Bighorn) Battlefield National Monument with my family. On that hot summer day, my wife Betty and son Michael, then four years old, were little inclined to walk the battlefield with me. So at the battlefield's visitors center, I stocked up on several books, including historian Robert M. Utley's *Custer and the Great Controversy* (Westernlore Press, 1962). It featured numerous footnote-level references to Kellogg and the role of newspapers in the campaign and its aftermath. Thanks to my journalism background, I found Kellogg intriguing enough to begin researching his life. Eventually, my biography of Kellogg was published under the title of *I Go With Custer: The Life and Death of Reporter Mark H. Kellogg*. I had quickly learned that to get to Kellogg I needed to go through Custer. Fortunately, many folks have been willing to assist in that quest, which remains ongoing.

Back in 1980, Utley pointed me toward the late John M. Carroll, the Custer buff par excellence, who, in turn, referred me to the late Leonard F. Kellogg. Leonard, a retired forestry professor at Iowa State University and a collateral descendant of Kellogg, turned out to be not only my most significant source of "Kelloggiana" but also a great friend. He, for example, pointed out some of Kellogg's own writings and I was able to add to that list.

Over the years, I befriended a number of staff members at Little Bighorn Battlefield National Monument. Through the kindness of former Superintendent Jim Court and later chief historian/acting superintendent Douglas McChristian, I spent multiple weeks on three occasions working at the battlefield in a media advisory role for the National Park Service during archaeological projects. That role afforded me many opportunities for close-up research in both the battlefield archives and on the field itself. Many of Court's successors, ranging from Gerard Baker to Neil Mangum to David Harrington, have been equally kind over the decades. Former chief historians, including Mangum, McChristian, and John Doernor, patiently answered my questions, offered their interpretations, and provided me with access to the collections. A number of permanent and seasonal rangers also have helped me. They include Dan Martinez, Doug Keller, Michael Moore, and Michael Donahue, the author of two important books on the battle. Former battlefield archivists Kitty Belle Deernose and Mark Nelson never complained, no matter how many times I asked for yet one more file or photo. Over the years, archaeologists Douglas D. Scott, now retired from the National Park Service, and Professor Richard A. Fox, now retired from the University of South Dakota, provided great assistance in interpreting historical events, both while I worked with them during the formal projects at the battlefield in the 1980s and more informally ever since then.

Many other researchers and historians have provided substantial assistance and advice across the years. Foremost among them have been my two battlefield "Pards," the late Brian C. Pohanka and Dr. James S. Brust. Historians Jerome A. Greene, Paul L. Hedren, and Gregory J. W. Urwin have been advisers over the years for numerous Civil War or Indian wars projects. Other friends who have contributed many times include Thomas Bookwalter, Jeff Broome, Rick Collin, Kevin Connelly, Darrell Dorgan, Dennis Fox, Kevin Galvin, Cliff Hamby, Reverend Vincent Heier, the late W. Donald Horn, Professor William Huntzicker, Dale Kosman, Michael Koury, the late Bruce Liddic, the late Frank Mercatante, Ronald Nichols, C. Lee Noyes, Gary Raham, the late Joe Sills, the late Glen Swanson, Francis Taunton, and Norvelle Wathen.

For many years while I was at Indiana State University, my three journalism colleagues in the Department of Communication, the late Dave Bennett, Michael Buchholz, and the late Paul Hightower, patiently listened to my tales of Custer, Kellogg, First Sergeant John Ryan, and Major Joel H. Elliott and offered writing and research hints. Business Professor Bruce McLaren served as a computer mentor and a great friend, even as I dished out far more information about Custer than he probably desired to learn.

Two other people deserve special note. My best friend, my wife, Betty, has not only willingly listened to all the tales that eventually made their way into my books and just as many that did not. She also has trekked across many miles of the "wilds" of various Civil War and Indian wars battlefields, picking up at least one tick on the way, and probably knows the backcountry of the Little Big Horn better than most Custer battle students and authors. She possesses a keen eye for detail, whether transcribing a Union officer's nineteenth century letter or helping me line up nineteenth century photos to reshoot for use as illustrations in my books.

In all of my forty years on the Custer trail, the best question

I have ever been asked remains one from our then eleven-year-old son, Michael. In June 1987, while accompanying me to the Little Big Horn for another round on the battlefield, he asked, "Dad, are we really going to spend seven more days here?" Almost a lifetime later, the answer has been yes, and still counting.

Of special note, each of my books has required the assistance of a wide variety of agencies, libraries, and individuals, who perhaps I should cite here if space permitted. I trust I properly thanked each of them in the acknowledgments in the respective works to which they made their greatest contribution. Still, I wish to acknowledge their assistance and thank them again for all their help.

Finally, I wish to thank former director Nancy Tystad Koupal and the editorial staff at the South Dakota Historical Society Press who have used their talents to markedly improve my manuscript. I deeply appreciate their assistance. Any errors or omissions, of course, are the fault of the author.

Preface

George Armstrong Custer's death and the defeat of the Seventh United States Cavalry Regiment on 25 June 1876 at the Battle of the Little Big Horn in faraway Montana Territory startled a nation preparing to celebrate its centennial anniversary during the Centennial Exposition in Philadelphia, Pennsylvania. Army leaders, in their first reaction to the news from the frontier, expressed skepticism that the seemingly indestructible "Boy General" of the United States Civil War, who had led dynamic cavalry charge after cavalry charge throughout the conflict, could have fallen in action at the hands of the Lakota and Cheyenne fighters.[1] The news soon proved true, assuring that Custer would forever remain more than a footnote in America's military legacy. While plenty of military heroes have emerged since the nation's founding, few have had as many words penned about them as this frontier officer.

History's opening encounter with Custer came in the Civil War when he became renowned for his enthusiastic cavalry attacks as commander of the Michigan Cavalry Brigade and the Union Army of the Potomac's Third Cavalry Division. At times, Custer's charges were challenging, if not reckless, and the young leader's men often sustained high casualties. Nonetheless, Custer contributed mightily to the Federal victory over the Confederacy between 1861 and 1865.

If the Civil War constituted act one in Custer's life, the period after the conflict became a more controversial, personal act two, in which Custer commanded the Seventh Cavalry as a lieutenant colonel for more than a decade on the Great Plains. Historians often stumble in crafting a suitable portrait of Custer the Indian fighter. On the plains, Custer and the Seventh Cavalry attacked American Indians, including the elderly, women, and children. In his time, white Americans viewed all Indians suspiciously, considering them untrustworthy and prone to committing violence. Modern society has largely rejected that notion as racist. Instead, tribal peoples of the nineteenth century are often viewed today as a patriotic minority who were sinned against as they attempted to defend their plains culture against an expansionist, Eurocentric population bent on their destruction.

Custer, a man of a distant nineteenth century with its different sensibilities, undoubtedly had few qualms about his military actions against American Indians. Although Custer spoke out against tribal mass destruction at times, in modern circles, he is often dismissed as an Indian hater and a symbol that is as out of step as Confederate memorials on southern village squares. His worst critics regard him as a man bent on genocide. His most significant victory in the West—a clash with Southern Cheyennes at the Battle of the Washita near the western border of modern-day Oklahoma in late November 1868—is dismissed as "a senseless massacre" of women, children, and elders. Similarly, his oft-criticized foray into the Black Hills in the summer of 1874 is considered to have accomplished little more than setting the table for what many view as his ultimate folly two years later at the Little Big Horn. Since his demise, according to author James S. Robbins, "Custer is talked about, written about, debated, loved, and hated" and has "come to symbolize tragedy, recklessness, valor, and disaster." No matter the view of these writers and historians, Robbins argues, "Custer the symbol has overcome Custer the man."[2]

It is that symbolic and legendary Custer that Americans puzzle over today. The facts of the Civil War, the Plains Indian wars, and Custer's actions do not change, although succeeding generations may reinterpret them. At his worst, Custer is forever reckless, courageous, egotistical, ambitious, brash, arrogant, and successful as a fighter. He can never leave that last-stand hill on the Montana battleground where a granite monument to him and his men has stood since 1881. Modern military veterans are often offered a handshake and a word of thanks for their service to their country. Custer and his Seventh Cavalry troopers are the symbolic exception in American military history. Because they campaigned against Indians under orders from the United States government, they must roam the plains in disgrace, seemingly forever.

For some three centuries before Custer was born, white European immigrants had settled and dominated most of what became the United States. Modern critics often see the nineteenth-century Custer as a scapegoat for the perceived and real evils that white settlers visited upon native peoples. The vast majority of those who settled in the West came to North America seeking not to conquer, but to take advantage of government policies to gain a better life for themselves and their families. Many were avoiding economic woes or were escaping religious or political persecution in their homelands. In that sense, they mirrored most immigrants throughout American history, including today.

Just like the white settlers in the West, American Indians were mystified by these strangers whose skin, customs, dress, languages, and expectations differed markedly from their own. They found little common ground with the European people who began to carve out new lives for themselves as if they already owned the lands where Indians had lived and roamed for centuries. Indian responses varied, as they had with other native populations for many centuries. They traded with some while fighting with others. They also stole property and kidnapped women and children, but many lived peacefully near white settlements as well.

By the time Custer himself ventured onto the Southern Great Plains in 1866 and 1867, most local Indian populations already endured severe stress on their nomadic lives. For many generations, plains inhabitants had effectively relied on a single resource—the buffalo. By the mid-1800s, those once vast herds were diminishing rapidly. White settlers and the United States government were pushing railroads and settlements across the country. Telegraph lines already tied the nation together and the telephone was a mere decade away. After the turn of the twentieth century, about a quarter century after the Little Big Horn, two more modern inventions would assure the closing of the frontier as Indians had known it. The automobile and truck would replace the horse and the wagon. People eventually could cross the plains in just a couple of days. The airplane would do motor vehicles one better, conveying people high above the plains in a matter of hours. Only a half century after Custer's death, modern tourists would travel from afar by car or plane to visit western national parks and historic sites, including Custer's own final battleground. Although Custer never saw the twentieth century, some of his indigenous adversaries lived deeply into it. How astounding they must have found such changes.

In 1866, with the Civil War concluded, Custer found himself at loose ends. What would he do for the rest of his life? Historians suggest he had trouble adapting to this next stage. As Robbins has stated, "There were fewer battles to be fought, less opportunity to give expression to his spirit." No longer part of a major conflict, Custer had to "reinvent himself while staying true to his character. It was a challenge he faced for the rest of his life."[3] That trial proved to be his last and greatest, and one that he never truly met.

In the last decade of his life, Custer never functioned as dynamically as his followers have claimed. Likewise, one lieutenant colonel hardly deserves the shameful responsibility for the near-demise of American Indians. Even in 1876, members of several tribes served as Custer's allies as he challenged their hereditary enemies, the Lakotas and Cheyennes.

This clash of cultures between whites and Indians in the late nineteenth century was far more complicated than the actions of Custer in his own final battle. The Lieutenant Colonel Custer on the Great Plains was far removed from the brevet Major General Custer who had mastered the Civil War battlefields in the eastern United States. Yet, Custer did not awaken one Sunday morning in late June 1876 and, on a whim, ride out of Fort Abraham Lincoln, Dakota Territory, intent on killing as many Indians as he could find that day.

While commanding twelve companies of the Seventh Cavalry during a six-week campaign, Custer was subordinate to another Civil War hero. Brigadier General Alfred H. Terry commanded Custer's horsemen as part of the Dakota Column, one of three that the federal government placed in the field that spring and summer to force so-called "hostile" Indians to move to reservations. Two other Civil War veterans and senior officers, Brigadier General George Crook and Colonel John Gibbon, commanded the Wyoming and Montana columns respectively. These three commanders were working under orders from their own superiors and the administration of President Ulysses S. Grant. With the benefit of today's hindsight, such orders appear flawed and even racist. Nonetheless, to the officers and soldiers of that era, it was a duty to be fulfilled.

By that campaign, the then thirty-six-year-old Custer ranked as no military has-been. It is worth noting that since the Civil War's end in 1865, he had commanded large bodies of troops in combat against an enemy only twice. The first was at the Battle of the Washita in 1868 and the second was in the summer of 1873 in minor skirmishes against Lakota warriors along the Yellowstone River in Montana Territory. Otherwise, Custer had spent the bulk of his eleven years since the Confederate surrender at Appomattox Court House, Virginia, as a garrison soldier. During the rebellion, he relied on his considerable battlefield acumen and his instinctive ability to maneuver experienced troops to great effect in combat. In addition, he had enjoyed a heavy dose of what his military comrades and newspaper reporters had dubbed as "Custer's Luck," referring to his knack for being in the right place at the right time and making the most of it.

General Nelson A. Miles defined it as Custer's natural judgment to do the right thing at the right time. His successes more often resulted from his ability to profit from an opportunity presented to him, something he did in both the Civil War and on the Great Plains.[4]

By the time of the Little Big Horn, Custer may have been fine physically, but he seemed less like the astute young officer who quickly sized up the battle action before him and responded immediately and brilliantly. He was now middle-aged, perhaps perceptively slower in thought and movement. He may even have been uncertain of his own next step, not having practiced his military craft for much of the postbellum era. Additionally, the men of the Seventh Cavalry were mere shadows of the soldiers in the Michigan Cavalry Brigade and Third Cavalry Division, units that many historians consider among the elite of the Union armies.[5] With some 40 percent of the Seventh's cavalrymen being recently arrived immigrants, many of the troopers lacked the requisite skills, combat training, and self-reliance they needed to stay alive and succeed on the plains.[6]

When operating on the plains, Custer and his officer peers shared a significant weakness. Their training and experiences had prepared them for fighting on contained battlefields similar to those that were commonplace in the Civil War. Yet, they falsely assumed that they understood how to fight Indians and how that new enemy would react in battle. They believed the Indians would always flee in the face of an armed force attacking their village and threatening their loved ones. That supposition on 25 June 1876 led Custer to implement standard tactics that he had used in previous engagements on the plains. He did not know that the confidence of his Lakota and Cheyenne opponents that day had probably swelled due to their numbers and what they considered a most successful engagement against George Crook's large command eight days before.

Finding the real Custer of the late 1860s and 1870s can

be daunting. For many decades, Custer's historical and symbolic significance had been little argued. Generations of white Americans who grew to maturity in the twentieth century and whose family lineages reach back into the eighteenth and nineteenth centuries are more and more passing away or, at least, are losing influence in modern society. Newer demographic groups are entering the discussion that the World War II generation and the Baby Boomers once dominated. New rounds of immigrants from Central and South America, the Middle East and Africa, and eastern Asia likewise are contributing to the increased diversity of the United States. As the authors of a 2014 demographic study reported in *USA Today*, "For the first time, the next person you meet in this country—at work, in the library, at a coffee shop or a movie ticket line—will probably be of a different race or ethnic group than you."[7] These newcomers may have little grasp of or strong interest in the previously familiar Eurocentric American history. They are changing how Americans live, study, learn, work, and worship together. They may question why they need to know anything about George Armstrong Custer.

For over half a century, both the Custer Battlefield Historical and Museum Association and the Little Big Horn Associates have dedicated themselves to studying the history surrounding Custer, whom they have viewed as one of the most successful and admired soldiers in United States history. In recent decades, however, their membership numbers have slumped. Today's typical member is an older white male with gray hair who likely presents a European background. With the myriad changes ongoing in American society, some fear that Custer himself may be making his own cultural last stand. These members even wonder whether Custer may finally recede into the footnotes of American history. Custer's vaunted luck failed him in 1876; symbolically, his mythical status may be slipping away as the country moves deeper into a more culturally diverse twenty-first century. As different groups venture onto the stage to play expanded roles in building American society in the years to come, they may rely far less on men such as Custer, who served their country to the best of their ability as America grew into a world power, as national symbols.

1 Early Life

George Armstrong Custer's life is clogged with mythical accounts of his actions and escapades. It all started in the Harrison County hamlet of New Rumley, Ohio, a town eleven miles from the county seat of Cadiz. New Rumley is where George, the third child of Emanuel H. and Maria Custer, was born on 5 December 1839.[1]

In 1823, Custer's mother, Maria Ward, a then sixteen-year-old tavern operator's daughter, had married Israel R. Kirkpatrick, a New Rumley merchant. In 1830, after Maria's parents and several other members of her family had died, the couple moved into her father's old tavern house. They had two children, David, born late in 1823, and Lydia Ann, born in 1825.[2]

Other members of the tight-knit southeastern Ohio community included its only blacksmith, Emanuel Custer. He had learned the blacksmith trade from either his own father, also named Emanuel, or his uncle, Jacob Custer, who had helped establish the hamlet in 1813. The younger Emanuel had arrived in New Rumley in 1824 and had gone to work in his uncle's shop.[3]

Emanuel succeeded Jacob in running the shop by 1828. He also had married Matilda Viers, the daughter of the town's justice of the peace. By 1833, the couple had three children, two sons Brice W., born in 1831, and John A., born in 1833, and an older daughter Hannah, who died within a year of her birth in 1830. Matilda herself died of natural causes in July 1835. With two children who needed additional care and still a young man himself, Emanuel would not be long in remarrying.

Four months earlier, Maria Kirkpatrick had lost her husband as well. Undoubtedly, in such a small town, Emanuel and Maria had known each other for years. About the same age and sharing the experience of a spouse's recent death, they were drawn to one another. On 23 February 1836, they married and took up residence in Maria's tavern house, which her first husband improved by adding a frame storeroom on the southeast side and clapboard siding. Just as tragedy frequently visited their previous families, it dogged their early years together as husband and wife. In July 1836, Emanuel's three-year-old son John died. Later that year, Maria gave birth to their own first child, James, but he too perished within a few months. In 1838, they lost a second son, Samuel.

Finally, in December 1839, George Armstrong was born in the back bedroom on the ground floor. An outgoing child with blue eyes and curly reddish-gold hair, George later was nicknamed "Autie" after mispronouncing his middle name while learning to talk. For the rest of his life, George Custer would be known as Armstrong or Autie to his family members and close friends. In the next decade, Maria gave birth to three additional sons and a daughter: Nevin Johnson (29 July 1842–25 February 1915); Thomas Ward (15 March 1845–25 June 1876); Boston (31 October 1848–25 June 1876); and Margaret Emma (5 January 1852–March 1910).[4] George was a devoted son, especially to his mother, described as "a woman of fragile health and strong maternal sensibility."[5] According to a recollection written late in life by his brother Nevin, Emanuel was "pretty strict: stricter than most fathers are nowadays, I guess."[6]

The blended family was close, probably because the parents were so different in their personalities. Historian Jeffry D. Wert refers to Maria as "the quiet, steady counterpoint to the loud, impulsive Emanuel."[7] To fellow historian Robert M. Utley, the Custers were "a high-spirited, rough-and-tumble family." Emanuel himself was "a man of firm conviction firmly expressed," one who espoused a militant brand of frontier Methodism.[8]

Emanuel worked the family farm the same way. "Everybody had his work cut out an' he had to do it without whimpering and do it promptly; sort of religious duty, yuh know, only I remember George hated to get his clothes smelly," Nevin recalled. "He and I made a dicker so that I did all the work at the barns while he split the wood and carried it in."[9] Custer mimicked his father in this regard. At times, Emanuel could be as much of a boy as his sons. Pranks, jokes, and fun-loving were the norm among the Custer males. Long after his sons' deaths at the Little Big Horn, Emanuel told George's widow, Elizabeth ("Libbie") Bacon Custer, "I was always a boy with my boys."[10]

According to both Nevin Custer and local writer Milton Ronsheim, Custer may have been a better student than his critics often allow. The latter stated, "Naturally bright, Armstrong hated to study. A remarkably rapid student, he did most of his studying in school, skimming over the lessons but making respectable marks."[11] Nevin recalled that George's younger brothers always "expected to grow up on the farm, but George didn't. He wanted to teach school right off." Nevin also noted that his older brother was always reading. Of course, he sometimes fooled his teacher, using his geography book to hide on top of his paper-back novels. "He use[d] to read 'em all the time in school, but the teacher . . . never caught him, for he was bright as a dollar and never missed a recitation."[12]

When George was about four years old, his father belonged to the local militia known as the New Rumley Invincibles. The youngster often attended the unit drills with his father. His brother recalled George being "a pretty good mascot," who wore a little uniform and carried a wooden gun that had been specially made for him.[13] Many Custer biographers have claimed that the unit's annual muster events provided the first stirrings of an interest in the military for the young

Custer.[14] Family friend John Giles suggested, "From that moment his passion to become a soldier originated and grew with his years."[15] That, of course, is a nice story to apply to Custer given his life's path, but he never suggested that experience was what launched him in that direction. Instead, more practical family considerations probably directed him to the United States Military Academy at West Point, New York, and his eventual army career.

Custer was exposed to various viewpoints and skills, thanks to his father's blacksmith shop. It served as a community gathering spot where patrons gossiped and exchanged political views. Emanuel, a Jacksonian Democrat, could expound on the political weaknesses of the Whig Party. Additionally, George had ample opportunities to ride horses while assisting his father.[16]

In 1849, however, Emanuel gave up his village blacksmith shop and moved the family to an eighty-acre farm in North Township about three miles northeast of New Rumley. The farm offered no more than a subsistence life, but the family persevered and worked it for a decade.

For the times, George was well-schooled compared to other children from the region. By 1852, the now twelve-year-old Custer had finished his six years of schooling that focused on reading, writing, and factoring, but his parents recognized that he, with his bright, inquiring mind, differed from their other children. He seemed destined for more than the often-harsh farming life of Harrison County. In 1846, Custer's half-sister, Lydia Ann Kirkpatrick, regularly described as a second mother to him, had married David Reed. Soon after, the couple moved to Reed's hometown of Monroe in southeastern Michigan.[17] In 1852, Monroe's schools offered better educational options for Custer than the more expensive high school in nearby Cadiz, so his parents determined to send him to live with the Reeds. That summer, Emanuel and George traveled to Monroe, where he would work for the couple in exchange for room and board.[18]

Custer lived with his half-sister and brother-in-law for about two years while attending the New Dublin School and then studied at the Young Men's Academy, run by Alfred Stebbins before it closed in 1855. Custer biographer Lawrence A. Frost writes that the young teen was "reliable and handy," helping Lydia around the house and keeping her company when she felt homesick.[19]

Custer scholars are uncertain about how strong a student he was in this more advanced period of his education. Jeffrey Wert speculates that Custer's "impulsive behavior and penchant for practical jokes continued" while in the Michigan schools. Even as Custer appeared attentive and respectful, Wert surmises, his "mind boiled with disruptive ideas."[20] No matter Custer's dedication to his schooling, Frost believed that Custer, who loved reading military novels, determined he would eventually seek an appointment to West Point while living in Monroe. "The Mexican War had just closed," Frost points out, "and most of the heroes had been West Pointers. It was enough to excite any military-minded boy."[21]

Many stories about Custer's life that sound apocryphal are frequently related in the extensive literature of Custeriana, making it difficult to separate the factual from the fanciful. One of those tales from his Monroe interlude concerns his first meeting with his future wife, Libbie Bacon. On this supposed occasion, Custer was on his way to school and passed the green-shuttered white house of Judge Daniel Stanton Bacon, Libbie's father.[22] Ahead of Custer was a pretty, dark-eyed girl who was swinging on her freshly painted picket gate. "As the boy passed," historian Milton Ronsheim records, "she said, smiling, 'hello! You Custer boy.' Then, frightened, she fled into her home."[23] Born on 8 April 1842, Bacon was only three years younger than Custer, who apparently remained smitten with her from that day forward.

In 1855 at fifteen years old, Custer returned to New Rumley. He now had two goals, to become a schoolteacher and to attend West Point. He taught at the Beech Point School and later at the Locust Grove School, both in Harrison County. In between terms, he attended McNeely Normal School in nearby Hopedale to improve his deficiency in mathematics, knowledge that could increase his chances of success if he were to attend West Point. Unfortunately for Custer, his local congressman, Representative John Bingham, had already filled his district's academy appointment for the upcoming school term.

The following year, Custer returned to McNeely and earned his formal teacher's certificate. He accepted a teaching position at District Number Five School in Cadiz Township, but he soon encountered controversy. While boarding with the family of Alexander Holland, he apparently fell in love with Holland's daughter Mollie. It is a mystery whether his feelings were fully reciprocated, but Holland was predictably upset to find that Custer had spent time in a trundle bed with his daughter and banished him from the house.[24]

On 27 May 1856, Custer sent a letter to Congressman Bingham as an application to West Point, but practical reasons stood in his way of acceptance. Custer's father was a Democrat while Bingham was a strong antislavery Republican in an age when political patronage influenced appointments to the academy. Although Bingham chose another candidate for that year, Custer was undaunted. He wrote a second letter that outlined his own unique characteristics. A month later, Custer found himself before the congressman for an interview at the latter's home in Cadiz. Many writers believe that Custer's subsequent appointment to West Point in 1857 may be considered "the first instance of 'Custer's Luck'." They suggest that Holland may have convinced Bingham to send him to New York for five years of schooling to remove the unwanted youthful suitor from his daughter's presence.[25] Whatever the case, Bingham nominated Custer in November 1856. Two months later, Secretary of War Jefferson Davis approved the appointment, which Custer accepted on 29 January 1857. Why Custer received his academy appointment matters little.

West Point would provide Custer with his ultimate career path. On 20 June 1857, sixty-eight plebes, or new cadets, arrived at the academy. As one of them, Custer was already a survivor. Earlier, 108 men had sat for an entrance examination, but 40 youths were dismissed out-of-hand as ill-prepared. That Custer, whose midwestern education was surely suspect compared to that of his eastern peers who received more elite schooling, had survived that first test and been admitted was remarkable. By June 1858, eight more of his classmates were gone. Two years later, Custer remained as one of thirty-five class members.[26]

Founded in 1802, West Point was hide-bound in its ways of producing the nation's army officers by the time Custer arrived more than fifty years later. Throughout the nineteenth century, an education from that institution "equaled or excelled that offered in most of the country's colleges and universities."[27] In the late 1810s, then-superintendent Sylvanus Thayer outlined an academic and military system designed to produce what existing officers considered the ideal skills for army commanders. Among the academic subjects central to the cadets' education preparation were language, mathematics, drawing, and a mix of history and liberal arts. On the military side, the cadets trained for placement in the engineering, infantry, artillery, or cavalry corps. What was most unwavering in their preparation for their careers was the strict discipline and regimentation of their daily lives. As Custer entered the academy in 1857, Jefferson Davis, an academy graduate himself, added a fifth year to the curriculum that Thayer had established.[28]

Much is made of Custer's academic struggles at West Point. As Robert Utley notes, Custer did not flourish in many of his classes. He had little motivation to study subjects that did not interest him. When he checked out books from the library, they usually featured "dashing cavaliers, flashing swords, and beautiful women."[29] By time his class graduated a year early in June 1861, only thirty-four cadets completed their studies and were eligible for commissions as second lieutenants in the army. Custer's status as his class goat—the student who ranked last—never seemed to bother him. Perhaps intuitively, he understood that one's academic record would matter little on the battlefield, nor would it handicap him much in the following decades of his life. Of course, for him, the latter idea would be moot, as he would not live to a ripe old age. Despite numerous interpretations that seek to account for Custer's defeat at the Little Big Horn, none has blamed his poor academic record. Still, some accounts use Custer's poor classroom performance at West Point to criticize him in general. For Custer, his academic rank never mattered.

If Custer's academics proved sufficient, his behavior was more suspect. Tully McCrea, who graduated in the official class of 1862, roomed with Custer during his own first year. To McCrea, Custer may have been "too clever for his own good. He is always connected with all of the mischief that is going on," he continued, "and never studies any more than he can possibly help."[30] As a cadet, Utley notes, Custer had "achieved considerable distinction at West Point, though hardly of the approved sort." Receiving one hundred demerits in six months resulted in a cadet's dismissal. Still, the academy's lengthy list of trivial regulations little concerned Custer, who accumulated demerits at a fast pace. Despite coming within 10 demerits on several occasions and earning a four-year total of 726, Custer survived.[31]

Custer's biographers generally credit him for his adeptness at more military-oriented tasks. He was a superb horseman, having had the chance to learn to ride as a child. In practice sessions, he also revealed his skill with using the saber. "In temperament as well as riding skills," Utley concludes, "he clearly belonged in the cavalry."[32]

Although not a model cadet, Custer enjoyed his life at

West Point. During his first encampment in the summer of 1857, Custer wrote a friend that he liked it more than he first expected, surprisingly calling it "the most romantic spot I ever saw." He even allowed that "military law is very severe and those who overstep its boundaries must abide the consequences."[33]

Given his record of infractions, this statement seems unusual, until looking at his time as a battlefield commander. Historian Louise Barnett best sums up Custer's personal inconsistency in that "the undisciplined cadet became a field commander who embraced a strict discipline." In school settings, the rules were set to control the youthful pupils. Such control measures had little tie to life's reality. For Custer, combat and the control of his troops in action became his immediate world for the next four years, starting virtually from the day he exited West Point. With Custer's military career beginning on the battlefield, where the value of discipline became immediately apparent, the "exceptionally young general, . . . wanted both officers and men to take him seriously."[34]

Custer apparently realized his limitations early at the academy. He was smart enough to survive his academic trials but had little interest in doing much more than that. With his carefree spirit, he was content merely to enjoy himself as much as possible. Nicknamed "Fanny" due to his long hair and fair complexion and "Curly" for his flowing locks, Custer was among the best-liked members of the corps. His peers made numerous positive comments about his personality, labelling him as fun-loving, personable, friendly, and popular. According to Wert, the other cadets saw in Custer a "spirit and zest for life that even the academy's disciplinary rigor could not smother." Throughout his studies, "He remained immature, and rebellious. Authority was meant to be tested, whether it was at a prayer meeting in the Monroe Methodist Church or at a drill on the Plain at West Point."[35]

Even as the country's political situation unraveled in

the late 1850s and early 1860s, Custer managed to remain friends with cadets from all sections of the United States. In April 1860 at the renowned off-post tavern Benny Havens, for instance, Custer organized a farewell party for five members of the class of 1860: Stephen Dodson Ramseur of North Carolina, John Pelham of Alabama, Thomas L. Rosser of Texas, Wesley Merritt of Illinois, and Henry du Pont of Delaware. One year after that evening of comradery, Ramseur, Pelham, and Rosser would face Merritt, du Pont, and Custer on the battlefields of the United States Civil War.

In June 1861, the conflict was already underway when the twenty-one-year-old Custer graduated as a member of the second class of 1861. Under the system of military appointments, the highest-ranking cadets at the time of graduation were destined to serve in the engineers, artillery, or ordinance. The lower ranking graduates were headed for the less glamorous branches of the infantry and cavalry. Despite Custer finishing last in the class of thirty-four, as an expert horseman, service in the cavalry was just fine for him.

The outbreak of the Civil War led army leadership to demand as many young officers as the academy could produce. Custer's record at the academy was not one to be celebrated. As the title of Utley's biography of Custer—*Cavalier in Buckskin*—suggests, the young officer undoubtedly lived outside of his properly designated time period. He must have belonged to a period when knights rode forth in shining armor with their lady's favor. As a fresh second lieutenant, he rode from the New York plains to join the United States forces at the battlefield of Bull Run near Manassas, Virginia. There, two inexperienced armies clashed and tested one another as cannons roared, destroying the unfortunate men and beasts who felt their explosive sting. Nonetheless, in this national strife, he would enjoy a spectacular rise to the rank of major general before the war ended four years later.

2 The Civil War

In discussing Custer's life, historians often refer to Custer's Luck. In the summer of 1861, his luck indeed held at the outset of his career. He avoided a severe setback when an academy board of officers court-martialed him for his failure to break up a fight between two cadets while acting as officer of the guard. It resulted in the army merely reprimanding him before sending him off to the emerging United States Civil War, where he led troops of the Second United States Cavalry Regiment during secondary fighting at the Battle of First Bull Run on 21 July. Custer and his comrades eventually became caught up in the routed Union army's chaotic retreat toward Washington, D.C. His first day of near combat brought no glory to the young lieutenant. He later noted that, during his quick twenty-five-mile ride from Washington to Centerville, Virginia, the night before, he had little expected to return with an army of "defeated and demoralized troops."[1] Bull Run showed that the conflict would be anything but brief, which meant Custer would yet find ample opportunities to make a name for himself.

After that initial fight, Custer was appointed as an aide-de-camp to Brigadier General Philip Kearny, then commander of the First New Jersey Brigade, for the summer and fall of 1861. The job, his first important assignment, pleased the junior officer. He wrote in his unfinished Civil War memoirs, "I found the change from subaltern in a company to a responsible position on the staff of a most active and enterprising officer both agreeable and beneficial."[2]

Kearny was a Mexican War hero who had lost his arm near the end of the earlier conflict. Custer described the promising commander in words that might well have referred to himself in both the Civil War and on the Great Plains. Of the many high-ranking officers with whom Custer served, Kearny was "the strictest disciplinarian. . . . a man of violent passion, quick and determined impulses, haughty demeanor, largely the result of his military training and life, brave as the bravest of men can be, . . . patriotic as well as ambitious, impatient under all delay, extremely sensitive in regard to the claims of this command as well as his own." As Custer viewed him, Kearny was also "distrustful of all those who differed with him in opinion or action, capable as a leader of men, and possessed of that necessary attribute which endeared him to his followers despite his severity." Custer believed that the general "presented a combination which is rarely encountered. He constantly chafed under the restraint and inactivity of camp life, and was never so contented and happy as when moving to the attack." He concluded that no matter how intense the action was, "Kearny was always to be found where the danger was greatest."[3]

With his habit of leading troops into the action, Kearny's fate came early in the war when he was killed on 1 September 1862 during the Battle of Chantilly or Ox Hill in Virginia.[4] As a young general, Custer would mirror many of the traits he attributed to Kearny. Custer would prove impulsive, impatient, and overly passionate about his duties. At the same time, he would demonstrate quick thinking, fearlessness, and courage. Most important, he never hesitated to act.

Despite meshing well with Kearny, Custer found his time on the general's staff "brief but agreeable."[5] That October, Custer fell ill and took a lengthy leave of absence that lasted until February 1862, spending that time in his adopted hometown of Monroe, Michigan. When it ended, Custer returned to his own unit, now redesignated as the Fifth United States Cavalry after Major General George B. McClellan reorganized the United States forces in Virginia, the newly designated Army of the Potomac. With the Fifth Cavalry, Custer began earning a reputation as a daring, resourceful young officer during the Peninsula Campaign between March and July 1862 in central Virginia. The operation was the Army of the Potomac's first major offensive in the Eastern Theater. McClellan successfully launched an amphibious movement that threatened the Confederate capital of Richmond. McClellan's campaign went smoothly while facing Confederate General Joseph E. Johnston, who was as cautious as his Union counterpart. In late May, however, Johnston was wounded and replaced by the more aggressive General Robert E. Lee. McClellan soon lost his edge and, by 4 August, he withdrew his army from the peninsula.[6]

As the Army of the Potomac first approached Richmond, Custer revealed his bold nature in combat. On 24 May, amid a morning rain, Lieutenant Nicholas Bowen, chief engineer for Brigadier General William F. ("Baldy") Smith, and Custer, acting as Bowen's assistant, headed a force of seventy-five soldiers from the Fourth Michigan Infantry Regiment. They led the foot soldiers to a ford site on the Chickahominy River that Custer had discovered earlier and waded across the waterway about three hundred yards above a road bridge known as New Bridge. Moving forward in skirmish line formation, they encountered the Fifth Louisiana and Tenth Georgia Infantry regiments and an artillery battery. Although outnumbered four to one, Custer and his men had the advantage of surprise. In the meantime, the remainder of their command formed a line perpendicular to the river and moved down toward the bridge.[7]

Sergeant Moses A. Luce of the Fourth Michigan later recollected the young lieutenant's heroics in what he called "the daring nature of the enterprise." Luce, who was later awarded the Medal of Honor for saving a wounded comrade on 10 May 1864 at Laurel Hill, Virginia, pointed out that the Bowen-Custer force lacked any artillery or infantry support in the face of these superior numbers. "The small force divided, — with a river between lined with swamps, — five hundred farmer's boys, unused to war and led by a youngster just from the Academy, were being dashed against this veteran brigade of valorous Southerners," Luce remembered. "But the boldness and decisive action of this born leader won a victory." Custer, who Luce described as "slender in build, with long flaxen hair and careless in dress," pushed his men rapidly down the river and surprised the enemy pickets. The Michiganders followed the fleeing Rebels "to their very camp opposite the bridge."

During the attack, Luce recalled Custer grabbing a "large bowie knife" from a Rebel prisoner. After Custer had "urged his horse across the stream," he rode to the head of the regiment and, while brandishing the weapon, he shouted, "The Rebels say we can't stand cold steel. I captured this from one of them. Forward and show them that the Michigan boys will give them all the cold steel they want." The Confederates fled as the rest of the Fourth Michigan dashed through the swamps and across the river, holding their bayonetted muskets above their heads until reaching the enemy's camp. The Southerners "fled routed from the valley." The Michiganders seized the bridge and thirty-five prisoners.[8]

McClellan rode rapidly through the rain to personally thank the officers and men for their victory and gallant conduct. McClellan called for the mud-draped Custer whom he described as "a slim, long-haired boy, carelessly dressed." The general shocked the lieutenant by appointing him as an aide-de-camp on his staff with the rank of captain. Recovering his demeanor, Custer replied that he "would regard such service as the most gratifying he could perform."[9] Custer had stepped forward from the shadows cast by thousands of other officers serving in the Army of the Potomac. His star was rising.

McClellan and Custer proved a favorable match. Throughout his military career, Custer was guilty of an almost childlike level of hero worship for some of his superiors. Libbie Custer understood this quality in her husband. She later noted, "Autie adored General McClellan. It was the hero worship of a boy."[10] McClellan also liked Custer. In an oft-repeated quote, the general described Custer as "simply a reckless, gallant boy, undeterred by fatigue, unconscious of fear; but his head was always clear in danger, and he always brought me clear and intelligible reports of what he saw when under the heaviest fire. I became much attached to him."[11]

Throughout the summer and into the fall of 1862, Custer remained on McClellan's staff, taking on numerous roles as the general's aide. Due to McClellan's inaction after the bloody Battle of Antietam on 17 September 1862, however, the axe fell on the commander. He was relieved of his post on 5 November, leaving Custer adrift without an assignment.[12]

While awaiting a new appointment, Custer returned to Monroe. During this period, Custer began to pursue a relationship with the woman who would, without question, be the most important influence in his life—Libbie Bacon. The young society girl would not be an easy conquest for Custer. She was attractive, well-educated, and highly personable with a bounty of friends, both male and female. She also could be highly judgmental about the boys who courted her. Custer's blonde hair, she had decided, was too light and even his military overcoat, lined with yellow trim according to army regulations, bothered Bacon. Ever eager to move forward, Custer agreed to tone down the offending yellows.[13]

Throughout that winter, the two young people sparred romantically, only slowly revealing the depth of their feelings for one another. Bacon often expressed her developing thoughts privately in her diary. Sometime early in the new year, Custer may have broached the subject of marriage, but she brushed him off as she was not ready for such a commitment.

Her father, Judge Daniel Bacon, proved an even more imposing obstacle to any potential relationship because he did not want his daughter to marry a soldier, especially this particular soldier after having witnessed a drunken escapade by Custer the year before. Custer's promise to avoid alcohol, which he did for the rest of his life, his status as a West Pointer, and his early lauded wartime army service may have somewhat boosted him in the elder Bacon's estimation. In early 1863, however, the judge still preferred that his daughter select someone from her own social circle. Despite her father's criticism of their relationship, Libbie refused to promise him that she would never see Custer again.[14]

In the spring of 1863, Custer pushed for a promotion and command of a regiment. He unsuccessfully sought a colonelcy and command of a Michigan unit from the state's governor, Austin Blair. In the meantime, Custer joined Mc-Clellan in New York City to assist the general in completing his reports on the previous year's operation. About the same time, Brigadier General Alfred Pleasonton, a Union cavalry leader, tapped Custer as an aide, setting Custer up for a bright future to become the famed "Boy General."[15]

The day of 28 June 1863 ranks as one of the most crucial in Custer's life. Achieving a general officer's rank may have been a life's dream for him, but on that day he learned that even in the midst of war dreams could come true. He found himself unexpectedly elevated to the rank of brigadier general and, with it, command of a full brigade of cavalry troops from his adopted home state, the Michigan Cavalry Brigade. His ascent was no simple matter of his personal brand of Custer's Luck. He had earned his promotion on the field of battle, time after time impressing his superiors with his boldness, courage, and dynamic thinking under severe pressure of enemy fire.[16]

For fifty-year-old Brigadier General Joseph T. Copeland, that day marked the end of his career as the Michiganders' commander. Although Americans had expected a short round of combat in April 1861, by the following summer, Lincoln and his generals acknowledged that the bitter and bloody fighting would continue indefinitely. In July 1862, Lincoln called for an additional three hundred thousand volunteers for three years of service. By that month, Michigan had already contributed sixteen infantry regiments, eight batteries of light artillery, and three cavalry regiments. In addition, the state was forming a fourth cavalry regiment and another infantry regiment. Following the president's order, the state would provide another twelve thousand men, assigned to six infantry and three cavalry regiments, the Fifth, Sixth, and Seventh Cavalry.[17]

In civilian life, Copeland was a well-known judge and attorney from Pontiac, Michigan, near Detroit. As a colonel, he helped raise the Fifth Michigan Cavalry in August 1862.[18] By early December, the regiment was encamped on East Capitol Hill in Washington, D.C., at a site the soldiers named Camp Copeland after their founding commander, about one mile from the Capitol Building. The state finalized raising the Sixth and Seventh Cavalry regiments in the months following the Fifth's organization. By February 1863, they were camped near the Fifth in Washington, D.C.[19]

A fourth cavalry regiment filled out the Michigan Cavalry Brigade. The more experienced First Michigan Cavalry had been created in August 1861 and was dispatched to join the Federal forces in Virginia in late September. During much of 1862, the unit engaged in extensive patrolling and fighting, often against the vaunted troops of Confederate Major General James Ewell Brown ("Jeb") Stuart.[20]

The Michigan Brigade, originally consisting of the three newer regiments, was officially organized under Copeland's leadership on 12 December 1862. For six months, the brigade remained tied to the defenses around the capital, most often serving on picket duty into the late spring of 1863. Throughout the winter, Union commanders worried that Stuart would launch raids against Washington as Colonel John S. Mosby's Confederate partisan troopers harassed Union pickets and launched raids behind Federal lines.[21]

In late June 1863, Copeland led the Fifth and Sixth Michigan, which had joined the Army of the Potomac in the field, on a scouting mission into Pennsylvania, seeking signs of

General Lee's Army of Northern Virginia. On 28 June, Copeland's troops entered Gettysburg, Pennsylvania, but found no signs of the enemy. According to the townspeople, Lee's army was split between the towns of Chambersburg to the west, Carlisle to the north, and York to the east.

Pleased at the success of his intelligence-gathering mission, Copeland and his troopers headed back to Emmitsburg, Maryland, expecting high praise from his superiors. Instead, a courier stopped Copeland and his staff enroute and informed him of changes occurring in the Army of the Potomac. The previous day, Major General George Gordon Meade replaced Major General Joseph Hooker, who had commanded the army since that January.[22] Meade immediately authorized widespread organizational and personnel changes. Among them, Pleasonton took over the cavalry corps and, essentially because he did not know Copeland, removed his Michigan subordinate from the post. In addition, Brigadier General Judson Kilpatrick was promoted to the head of the Third Cavalry Division, consisting of two brigades. A newly appointed brigadier general, Elon J. Farnsworth, one of Pleasonton's former staff officers, would lead its First Brigade. Brigadier General Custer would take over the Second Brigade, now consisting of the Michigan Cavalry Brigade's legendary wartime alignment with all four regiments. For the next fifteen months, Custer would brilliantly command these troops.

After taking command of his new unit, Custer connected with only a portion of his brigade. Late in the afternoon of 29 June, Custer met the First and Seventh Michigan at their encampment near Frederick, Maryland. He soon led his small contingent, including a battery of artillery, north and then northeast to Littlestown, Pennsylvania. Meanwhile, the Fifth and Sixth remained with Copeland on his final reconnaissance.[23]

That evening, the Michiganders camped with the First Brigade only a dozen or so miles away from three Confederate cavalry brigades under Jeb Stuart. Probably no more colorful character existed in the Army of Northern Virginia than Stuart. Earlier in the war, he led both foot and horse soldiers, but his specialty became the cavalry. For almost two years, Union horsemen failed to compete equally with the dashing and aggressive Stuart. Barely a few weeks before, on 9 June at the Battle of Brandy Station, Virginia, Federal cavalrymen smashed Stuart's seeming invincibility on the battlefield. He was startled to find that the Yankees had rapidly closed the performance gap. Pleasonton's cavalry troopers stung Stuart in that battle. For the Rebels, Brandy Station "was certainly a rude blow across the face of Southern pride and reputation."[24]

In response to this recent setback, Stuart and his cavalrymen tried to circle the Army of the Potomac, as he had done in the Peninsula Campaign, creating havoc and mischief wherever he surfaced for several days. At Rockville, Maryland, his units captured 125 Union wagons as they rode back toward Lee's army. With Federal troops between him and Lee, Stuart could not provide Lee with crucial intelligence about the enemy's movements. Both Confederate leaders faced serious problems while deep in Union territory. Lee, without Stuart, effectively operated without his army's eyes. Stuart, despite trying to avoid Union cavalry, kept encountering the enemy, turning his plan into "an eight-day ordeal that quickly became a nightmare . . . of agonizing marches and hard fights that strained to the limit the very fiber of the Confederate cavalryman."[25]

The morning of 30 June, the Fifth and Sixth Michigan joined Custer and the other two regiments. As rain fell, the two brigades of Kilpatrick's Third Cavalry Division headed toward Hanover, Pennsylvania, while screening the Army of the Potomac. When they arrived, grateful residents turned out with food to share with the men.

Stuart's men, still encumbered by more than one hundred captured wagons, were also on the move with the goal of linking up with Lee's army, not clashing with the enemy's cavalry. As they approached Hanover, Stuart realized Union cavalry units blocked his path. He ordered his leading brigade to charge Farnsworth's Yankees. At first, the Southerners drove back the Union troops, but a Federal counterattack forced Stuart's men to retreat.

Soon after, Kilpatrick arrived with Custer and his brigade, taking up a position on a rise north of Hanover known as Bunker Hill. About the same time, the Fifth and Sixth Michigan Cavalry engaged a Confederate brigade under Colonel Fitzhugh Lee, the nephew of Robert E. Lee. The two Michigan regiments held their own for a time but retreated shortly after while a squadron of the Sixth provided effective cover with their multi-shot Spencer rifles. The two units rejoined Custer, giving him some twenty-three hundred men under his command. For the rest of the afternoon, the two sides engaged one another across the farmlands outside Hanover with neither side managing to dislodge the other despite repeated assaults. The outnumbered Stuart opted to break off the fighting and continue to try to locate the main Rebel army.[26]

To his credit, Custer's new command performed well in its first action under him. Despite the Fifth, Sixth, and Seventh having "smelled battle smoke for the first time," only the Sixth and Seventh Michigan had fallen back during the fight. Even then, the brigade ultimately stood firm and kept the enemy at bay, forcing Stuart into what he likely considered an unnecessary fight that delayed his real objective.[27]

By the following morning, the Confederate cavalry was no longer in sight and the massive armies of Meade and Lee streamed toward Gettysburg, initiating one of the Civil War's most momentous battles. Although the first day's fighting went poorly for the Army of the Potomac, the soldiers managed to regroup on the ridges and hills south of town. Meade decided to stand and fight, ordering the cavalry to come to him on 2 July. By mid-afternoon, Kilpatrick received orders to guard the army's right flank on the north end of the battlefield. With Custer's brigade in the lead, the division settled along a narrow country lane where the Sixth Michigan clashed with Confederate pickets.[28]

After the clash at Hanover, Stuart continued eastward. By the morning of 1 July, after a fitful night of marching and sleeping in the saddle, his troops had lost Kilpatrick. Later that day, they engaged Pennsylvania militia troops near Carlisle, twenty-five miles north of Gettysburg. After that fight, Stuart finally encountered a bit of good luck. A courier from Lee, while searching for Stuart, ran into him with news of the Confederate army's whereabouts. Although much of Stuart's mounted force was worn out after days of marching, fighting, and searching, he managed to corral his scattered brigades and direct them toward Gettysburg on 2 July. Stuart himself headed for Lee's headquarters near the Lutheran Seminary on the western outskirts of town, arriving there around midnight. Lee reportedly was alternately angry at Stuart for his absence and pleased that his cavalry had finally returned. Lee ordered Stuart to post his three brigades on the Confederate left flank unknowingly placing them opposite Custer and the Third Cavalry Division.[29]

Earlier that day, elements of the Federal cavalry division challenged Rebel horsemen under Brigadier General Wade Hampton near Hunterstown, five miles northeast of Gettysburg. Hampton advised his superior of this new threat and moved his brigade toward the town to counter the Union advance. The town lacked any military value, except for a network of five roads that "controlled access to the Confederate left flank and rear at Gettysburg."[30]

About 4:00 PM, units of the Michigan Cavalry Brigade found Hampton's brigade occupying Hunterstown and soon engaged in a sharp fight that included a detachment of Custer's Sixth Michigan Cavalry. The Federals forced the Southerners to retreat, but they soon joined some comrades at a nearby farm. Kilpatrick and Custer had no idea how many Confederates were now before them. Still, Kilpatrick ordered his subordinate to charge the enemy. After posting his artillery on a knoll to support his troops, Custer had the First and Seventh Michigan dismount while the Sixth Michigan took positions among the buildings of another farm. The Fifth remained mounted in reserve. The road by which the attack would be made was hemmed in by fences and fields of wheat and corn, a less than ideal place for cavalry to charge a well-prepared enemy.

As Company A of the Sixth Michigan prepared for the attack, Custer rode forward to take the lead of the column. Behind the attacking force, other elements drawn from his brigade posted themselves within the confining fences and fields. Unknown to Custer, the Rebel troops of Colonel Pierce M. B. Young, another friend of his at West Point, stood in front of him. When they separated at West Point, Young predicted the two would clash on the field of battle. That moment almost proved to be a personal disaster for Custer.

The Georgians under Young first scattered as Custer led the Sixth Michigan troopers down the road, but they soon rallied. At one point, Custer's horse was shot out from under him. One of his privates, Norvill F. Churchill of the First Michigan, wounded a Confederate soldier just as he took aim at the fallen Custer. Pulling Custer onto his own horse, the private dashed to safety with his freshly minted general riding behind him. The Michiganders soon retreated as the Confederates won the engagement. The Rebels followed until receiving fire from the reserve troopers. As daylight faded, Hampton withdrew his men.[31]

While Kilpatrick praised Custer's Michiganders, the twenty-three-year-old general's own rashness nearly proved fatal in his first serious engagement as a brigade commander. Historian Gregory J. W. Urwin colorfully describes Custer's experience as ending "like a snowball thrown against a brick wall."[32] The young brigadier displayed more immaturity than capability at Hunterstown. Although the

Michigan Brigade's two engagements had not been unqualified successes, Custer's troops held their own against a more experienced enemy. He could take solace in the fact that he impressed his men by leading them from the front. His next action in command would not be long in coming.

Even though the second day of fighting at Gettysburg had been one of the more vicious, brutal days of the conflict, Meade expected the battle to resume the next day, 3 July. He repositioned his troops, including his cavalry, to strengthen the center of his line. Kilpatrick's division was ordered south toward the Union's left flank at a large hill named Big Round Top, halting for the night at the small community of Two Taverns. On that morning, before Custer set his unit in motion, Pleasonton directed Custer's brigade to support Brigadier General David M. Gregg's Second Cavalry Division, which was protecting the northern flank and rear of the Army of the Potomac. After Custer arrived, Gregg positioned the Michigan Brigade near the intersection of Hanover and Low Dutch roads, important avenues for the army if it had to withdraw. Gregg faced a serious problem as he had only two of his brigades present, both of which were well-worn and below strength after seeing considerable fighting.

The whole area along the right flank largely consisted of farm fields surrounded with fence lines and woods. A small creek, Little's Run, rose from a springhouse on the nearby Rummel family farm and flowed south toward Custer's position. Beyond the Rummel property, the mostly wooded Cress Ridge ran north for a mile. Custer arrived on the field just before ten o'clock that morning but had little time to wait for his next round of action.

Stuart's cavalry had been holding the Rebel's left flank and was advancing toward Cress Ridge. At the same time, eleven Confederate infantry brigades along Seminary Ridge to the west prepared to storm the Federal middle on Cemetery Ridge in a massive attack that became known as Pickett's Charge. To assist the infantrymen, Stuart had designs on disrupting the Union line from the rear. Cannon fire from Cress Ridge announced Stuart's own arrival on what would be named East Cavalry Field, but for a couple of hours neither side made a significant move toward the other.

Late in the morning, Major Peter Weber of the Sixth Michigan Cavalry alerted Custer that Stuart's troopers were massing along Cress Ridge. A second message for Custer arrived shortly after with more startling news. Kilpatrick wanted him to rejoin the Third Cavalry Division on the southern flank. Gregg received similar orders, but other reports warned both men that Stuart was about to attack. Gregg and Custer agreed that the Michigan Brigade should remain in place.

With action looming before him, the "Boy General" could not have been more pleased to stay. He positioned his regiments along Hanover Road again and placed Lieutenant Alexander Pennington's artillery battery to their front. The Sixth Michigan deployed four dismounted companies while the rest remained mounted and positioned to protect Pennington's men. The Seventh Michigan moved to the right to both support the ordinance line and act as a mounted reserve. The First Michigan formed in the center while the Fifth Michigan dismounted and, with their multi-shot Spencers, went forward as skirmishers. Essentially, the Michigan Brigade would bear the initial brunt of any Confederate advance.[33]

Gregg, as overall commander, finalized the Union line by placing his own units in the formation. Except for artillery fire, little was happening on this field. About one o'clock that afternoon, however, all the troopers heard the blasts and felt the rumblings of the artillery dual between the Confederate and Union cannons on Seminary and Cemetery ridges to the west. Captain James Kidd recalled, "The tremendous volume of sound volleyed and rolled across the intervening hills like a reverberating thunder in a storm."[34]

By two o'clock, the cavalry action began to heat up. Two

regiments from Gregg's units moved forward toward the Rummel farm. They soon met a brigade of Virginia horsemen. To assist the two regiments, Custer ordered the Fifth Michigan to advance. They took up a position behind a stake-and-rail fence and the Sixth Michigan moved in on their right along Little's Run.

With the advantage of their Spencer rifles, the Fifth Michigan forced back the Third and Ninth Virginia Cavalry. Another massive mounted charge by the Ninth Virginia momentarily scattered the Union regiments, including the Fifth Michigan whose Spencers quickly rushed through their ammunition supply. In response, Gregg ordered the Seventh Michigan to charge. As the regiment readied for the attack, Custer galloped forward. He would again lead one of his units in its charge, this time yelling above the din, "Come on, you Wolverines." The assault was brilliant initially, but the fence line the Fifth Michigan previously held slowed the Michiganders. They and the Virginians clashed along the fence like two heavyweight boxers in a grudge match. Troopers from both sides punched and counterpunched with their sabers and pistols.

Even then, Stuart dispatched additional Confederate regiments into the fray. In the midst of all this chaos and death, a Michigan officer fell wounded in front of Private Steven Gaines of the Fourteenth Virginia Cavalry.[35] Gaines asked the Yankee who his leader was and learned it was Custer. Forty-three years later, Gaines wrote Custer's widow and related the story. He told Libbie, "That was the first time I had ever heard his name, but, afterwards, I had occasion to become very familiar with it."[36]

As the Seventh Michigan began to bend under the pressure, one of Gregg's brigade commanders, Colonel John B. McIntosh appeared and urged them to hold their line. Colonel Russell Alger, who gained command of the Fifth Michigan just a few weeks before, dispatched two of his companies forward in support. McIntosh's own dismounted troopers fired on the Rebels as they appeared. Soon, the Southerners retreated to the safety of the woods along Cress Ridge, allowing the Seventh Michigan to regain the protection of the Union guns.

The Confederates' own retreat was only temporary. After the back and forth fighting had not given either side a clear-cut edge, eight regiments of Wade Hampton's troopers appeared in front of the Cress Ridge woods determined to force the Yankees to flee. With sabers raised, they directed their assault on Gregg's men holding the center.[37] Several days later, Captain Kidd described the scene in a letter to his parents. "On came the Rebel cavalry, yelling like demons, right toward the battery we were supporting apparently sweeping everything before them," he recorded. "Even though Union artillery created havoc among the oncoming Southerners, their charge barely slowed."[38]

The Michigan regiments were not in a good position to face the assault at the moment. The Seventh was still scattered. The Fifth remained largely on foot, looking for their horses. The Sixth was required to defend Pennington's Battery. Only the First Michigan stood ready to challenge Hampton's legions. Following Gregg's orders to answer the charging Confederates, the First Michigan's commander, Colonel Charles H. Town, who was seriously ill with consumption, somehow managed to mount his horse. Immediately, Custer joined the ailing colonel at the head of his regiment.[39] When the two forces were about one hundred yards apart, Union cannon fire sprayed the Confederate front, noticeably slowing it. At that moment, Custer again yelled, "Come on, you Wolverines," and charged, saber pointed at the enemy. The vicious battle was enjoined for five to ten minutes. In addition, troopers from two of Gregg's regiments lunged forward and struck the Rebels from the sides, while the other Michigan Brigade regiments rallied. With Hampton wounded and falling back, the Southerners rode furiously for the safety of Cress Ridge. The Northerners were also spent and the fighting melted away.[40] In a letter to his sister, Custer expressed his thrill over the Union victory. "I challenge the annals of warfare," he wrote, "to produce a more brilliant or successful charge of cavalry" than what the First Michigan had accomplished that day.[41]

Federal casualties were high with 254 troopers killed, wounded, or missing. On the other side, the Confederates lost 181 men. The Michigan Brigade's own casualties numbered 29 dead, 123 wounded, and 67 missing. Just as the cavalry clash came to a close, the Yankee infantry on Cemetery Ridge repulsed Pickett's Charge, ending Lee's final effort at breaking their lines. Historian Gregory Urwin observes, with both the Confederate infantry and cavalry bloodied and beaten, "The Battle of Gettysburg was over, and thanks to George Armstrong Custer and his Michigan Cavalry Brigade, as much as to any other commander and command in the Army of the Potomac, it was a Union victory" in what would come to be seen as the watershed event of the conflict.[42]

At the time of Custer's appointment as a brigadier, twenty-year-old Second Lieutenant Edward G. Granger of Company C in the Fifth Michigan Cavalry was stuck on his own backwater assignment guarding the supply train for the Michigan Brigade and missed his new commander's debut in the hard fighting at Gettysburg. For much of the post-Gettysburg campaign, Granger commanded his company as the brigade's provost guard and rode closely with Custer. On 20 August 1863, Custer appointed Granger as an aide-de-camp on his brigade staff.

In a letter from early September 1863, Granger could not hide his boyish enthusiasm from his sister, Mollie, after the general named him "to my present brilliant position." He called it a "very pleasant position, indeed, as the General is one of the most perfect Gentlemen I have met in the Army." Granger also expected to be much more involved in combat than before. "In battle, when we get into one, I suppose we shall have a chance to show the stuff we are made of as Gen.

Custer is one of the 'fighting Generals' of whom we read so much and see so little."

Granger next described the appearance of his new general. According to Granger, Custer was a "young man of three and twenty, nearly six feet tall and well made, complexion red, eyes blue, hair yellow and hanging in curls on his shoulders, mustache & imperial of the same elegant color." He continued that the general "dresses in velveteen with an indefinite number of yards of gold-lace on the sleeve of his jacket as an indication of his rank, but when dressed for review makes by far the most splendid appearance of any officer I have seen,—morals West Point—manners perfect—temperament lively & full of fun."[43]

After Gettysburg, the Union and Confederate forces settled in on either side of Virginia's Rappahannock River to recover from the bloody campaign. By September, however, the two armies stirred once again. As part of an advance by the Army of the Potomac, Pleasonton ordered his ten thousand man corps across the river to attack Stuart's headquarters at Culpeper Court House, Virginia, on 12 September 1863. During the following day's battle, Custer and the Michigan Brigade charged headlong into a line of artillery that was causing havoc for the Third Division. In the attack, the unit captured one hundred prisoners and three cannons, but Custer was also hit with shrapnel from artillery fire. An exploding shell killed his horse and a piece tore through his boot, leaving him with a nasty contusion. Despite the injury, Custer jumped onto another mount and continued leading the brigade in its pursuit, capturing Stuart's headquarters as the Rebels fled through the streets of Culpeper Court House. For his injury, Custer received twenty-days leave.

Custer and many of his troopers took the opportunity to go home to Michigan during those twenty days. They returned to the Army of the Potomac in time to take part in the Bristoe Campaign of October 1863. That month, Lee tried one last offensive to put his army between the Union forces and Washington, D.C., but the Rebels quickly retreated after suffering defeat in a brief, bloody fight at the Battle of Bristoe Station on 14 October. With winter beginning to set in, both armies went into camp, creating a lull in the conflict.[44]

The early months of 1864 proved significant for the young general. In his personal life, Custer continued to work on winning over Libbie and Daniel Bacon for much of 1863. Eventually, by late that fall, Libbie had accepted him. Judge Bacon soon followed, probably now influenced by the prospect of having a general in the family. At first, Libbie wanted to wait a year to marry, but they set 9 February 1864 for their nuptials. Some three hundred guests overflowed the First Presbyterian Church of Monroe for the wedding.

After the ceremony, the Custers went on tour, visiting members of Libbie's family in upstate New York and eventually West Point. While there, George was greeted as a distinguished alumnus. At one point, Custer left his bride alone, but not for long as cadets and professors soon surrounded the pretty young woman. When the two boarded their train for the final leg to New York City, a jealous George expressed his unhappiness with all the attention Libbie had received at the academy. She dismissed his concerns by reminding him, "Well, you left me alone with them, Autie." Editor Marguerite Merington claimed that, according to Libbie, this was the only occasion in which George displayed any jealousy involving her.[45]

After a brief stay in New York City and a pleasant round of dinners and theater in Washington, D.C., the general returned to the army. With Libbie joining him, the Custers traveled to brigade headquarters at Stevensburg, Virginia. George easily resumed his role as an army general. At West Point, Libbie had gained a sense of Custer's standing as "a man of distinction."[46] In Stevensburg, she found herself overwhelmed by army life at first. She had surrendered the sheltered life and comfort of a home in Monroe, far from the war, for the hustle, bustle, and mud of an army encampment near the front. More important, she lacked female companionship, except for their housekeeper whom she called the "blessed, black angel Eliza."[47] The Custers may have wished to be together but, from a modern perspective, it was probably a poor decision to subject Libbie to such turmoil and possible danger. Likely, George showed little concern because he wanted to be with Libbie. Later, living on the frontier, he would expose her to peril again.

After Custer set off on his first post-wedding operation, Libbie described being "completely overwhelmed with intense anxiety for my husband, bewilderment over the strange situation, and terror of the desolate place." She also feared her proximity to "the Southern family who could have no feeling but hostility toward the invading 'Yankee,' though they depended upon us for food." Eliza sought to reassure the young wife, telling her, "He'll come back, Miss Libbie. He always does you know. Didn't he tell you he'd come back?"[48] While Libbie may have appreciated Eliza's sentiments, she understood how the vagaries of warfare could render any loved one's promise to return worthless in a moment.

The second noteworthy event in Custer's life that spring, on a professional level, involved more personnel changes in the Army of the Potomac. On 2 March 1864, President Abraham Lincoln promoted Ulysses S. Grant, who had built an impressive combat record in the Western Theater, to lieutenant general, giving him command of all Union armies with only the president overseeing him. No other commander except for George Washington had been handed such authority as Grant held and he set out to shape the Federal forces according to his preferences. Near the end of the month, Grant established his personal headquarters with Meade's Army of the Potomac, which remained in winter camp near Culpeper, Virginia.[49]

The Army of the Potomac officially remained Meade's command, but Grant took a series of actions to convert it into the fighting force that he desired. He reorganized the infantry corps, for example, eliminating the I and III Corps that had borne heavy casualties in 1862 and 1863. He reassigned the surviving troops to the remaining II, V, and VI Corps. During this reorganization, Grant also planned a multi-front assault against all the Confederate forces. Engaging all the Rebel armies, he believed, would prevent them from moving personnel and supplies among the different theaters, weakening their overall efforts.[50] Grant's actions essentially defined the crucial ways he differed from his Confederate counterpart Robert E. Lee. Grant biographer Ron Chernow considers Lee "a master tactician" in individual battles but points out that Grant "excelled in grand strategy." While Lee was "stuck to Virginia," Chernow argues, Grant "grasped the war in its totality, masterminding the movements of all Union armies."[51]

One of Grant's decisions, however, terminated the strong tie between Pleasonton and Custer. The former was transferred to the Trans-Mississippi West, where he would perform capably as commander of the District of Central Missouri and District of Saint Louis. In an 1880 interview, Pleasonton expressed admiration for his former subordinate. "He was a splendid leader, and when he was upon my staff he did some wonderfully brilliant things," Pleasonton stated. He also praised the Boy General for being a "splendid horseman, fearless, graceful and dashing."[52] Yet, Pleasonton's own issues severed his connection with Custer. According to historian Jeffry Wert, Pleasonton "rejuvenated the mounted arm" but he had not been "a brilliant commander."[53] Additionally, his frequent administrative complaints had irritated Meade and other Washington authorities. No matter how personal the decision to send Pleasonton west may have been, Grant was surrounding himself with men who understood his thinking.

To replace Pleasonton, Grant turned to one of his infantry commanders from the Western Theater, Major General Philip H. Sheridan.[54] Grant viewed Sheridan as an aggressive combat officer, who would make up for his lack of cavalry experience by demanding his men to perform or answer to him in his firm, unforgiving manner. Initially, the change in his commanders disappointed Custer as did his own failure to be named a divisional commander. He told his sister in a letter on 23 April, however, that "Gen. Sheridan from what I learn and see is an able and good commander and I like him very much."[55]

Under Sheridan, Custer contributed mightily to the Federal victory in April 1865. As part of the Cavalry Corps in early 1864, Custer and his Michigan Brigade participated in raids against Confederate supply routes to disrupt the war effort. One of these attempts, the two-day Battle of Trevilian Station, almost ended in disaster for the young general in what Civil War historians often label as Custer's First Last Stand. Trevilian Station was a stop along the Virginia Central Railroad, which ran directly to the Rebel lines around Petersburg and Richmond. Capturing it would disrupt the flow of matériel to the Army of Northern Virginia. Between 9 and 11 June, the Union cavalry, including Custer's brigade, advanced on the station and found Rebel horsemen under Wade Hampton and Fitzhugh Lee.

Early on the morning of 11 June, the Confederate forces attacked Union troopers under Brigadier General Alfred Torbert and Custer. While the First and Seventh Michigan repulsed the enemy troops, Custer received reports of a massive Confederate wagon train nearby. That prize was too much for the energetic Custer to ignore. He immediately ordered the Fifth and portions of the Sixth Michigan, which had been delayed by rough terrain, to charge the Rebel troops and wagons. The men of the Fifth returned with as many as 350 prisoners, some 250 wagons, and about 1,000 horses.[56]

Although seemingly flush with success, neither Custer nor any of his subordinates recognized that the enemy cavalry threatened them from all sides. In only a matter of moments, two Confederate divisions had penned in his units and were poised to overrun his vaunted brigade. At one point, the commander of Custer's wagon train asked the general whether he should move it to the rear. Custer gave his assent, but then blurted out, "Where in hell is the rear?" The question had no answer.[57] The unknown officer drove the wagons off right into the hands of the Rebels. The items lost included Custer's love letters to Libbie. Some of their content ended up being published in the Richmond newspapers.

His early over-eagerness to seize the enemy's wagons created the nearly disastrous situation in which Custer had found himself and had thoroughly stressed his brigade through a day of frantic fighting. As Major Kidd summarized with comments that fit the entire brigade, "This regiment was engaged the entire day, fighting both mounted and dismounted, charging and counter-charging. Not less than one hundred prisoners were captured by the regiment, but being surrounded for several hours, many men were necessarily lost."[58] Still, the young general kept a cool head throughout. He led his men in a counterattack trying to break out of the trap and even saved the brigade's colors as the color bearer, Sergeant Mitchell Beloir, had been mortally wounded.[59]

Custer's casualties during the more than three hours of fighting soared. Some 416 soldiers of the brigade were lost, including 41 killed and 242 captured. The enemy had seized nearly half of the Fifth Michigan Cavalry. Custer must have grown miffed that help had not yet come to him, but about noon, Sheridan directed Torbert to have Merritt's and Devin's brigades fight their way through the encircling Confederates to rescue their nearly exhausted comrades. That counterattack forced Hampton to withdraw his own tired troops, ending what would prove to be just the first of two days of fighting.[60]

Custer overestimated his own capabilities that day at Trevilian Station, but he was not alone. Going into battle,

Hampton did not expect to meet such fierce resistance from the Union cavalry. He also had been stunned when Custer initially seized his supply wagons. Sheridan and his subordinates, on the other hand, were surprised that one of their brigades had been surrounded in a near slaughter pen and that the Confederates fought so ferociously to keep the relief troops at bay for so long.[61]

That day's fighting essentially ended in a draw. Sheridan's command camped on the Trevilian Station battlefield. For their part, the Confederates controlled the railroad tracks east and west of the station. The next afternoon, Sheridan sought victory again, but seven assaults all failed to dislodge the now consolidated line of Hampton's troops. Although the second day's fighting was almost more desperate, Custer's brigade played a lesser role in the action.[62] Once the fighting closed, the Yankee cavalrymen returned to White House Landing on the Pamunkey River, where the Federals had established their supply base for the upcoming nine-month siege of Petersburg, Virginia.

Despite Custer facing embarrassment after his near disaster at Trevilian Station in June, two months later he received an opportunity to redeem himself as he and his brigade joined Sheridan's newly formed Army of the Shenandoah in August 1864. Under orders to drive the Confederates out of the lush Shenandoah Valley, Sheridan was told that his soldiers should take whatever provisions, forage, or stock they needed. Otherwise, "such as cannot be consumed, destroy."[63] On 10 August, Sheridan initiated the movement up the valley.

Five days later, the Federals confronted the main Confederate force under Major General Jubal Early. On 14 August, Sheridan learned that Lee was sending infantry and cavalry reinforcements to Early. That evening, Sheridan dispatched Colonel Thomas Devin's brigade beyond Front Royal, Virginia, and into Chester Gap to look for these additional Southern troops.

The following day, Custer's brigade, sent to join Devin's men in that effort, reached them near Front Royal early in the afternoon and encamped a mile above the waterway, Crooked Run. With Custer in overall command, the two Union officers prepared for any eventuality, even though no enemy troops had yet appeared. The action quickly developed on 16 August as Confederate infantry and cavalry under Major General Richard H. Anderson appeared along the main road to Front Royal. About 3:00 PM, the Southerners launched their attack and drove the Yankee's picket line back toward Crooked Run, which historian Scott C. Patchan calls "the defining geographic feature of the developing battle."[64] For a time, the Confederates successfully advanced and controlled the heights with their artillery. Outnumbered, the Union troops fell back slowly over the creek, all the while continuing to fight.

Meanwhile, word reached Custer about the enemy's advance and the retreat of the Union pickets. Within ten minutes, he had his Michigan Brigade ready for action as he stood on a piece of high ground surveying the rugged battlefield before him. Holding the ridges and ravines around the road, Custer's brigade, especially the Fifth Michigan, ripped apart two Confederate regiments that charged into the Federal line. In the midst of the action, Custer, who had moved closer to the brigade's position, suddenly seemed to grab at the side of his head. Fortunately, a Confederate bullet had merely clipped off one of the general's golden ringlets, dropping it to his shoulder. Just then, Custer launched a counterattack that broke the Rebel advance, pushing the broken units back across Crooked Run.

Historian Gregory Urwin labels the Crooked Run battle "one of the most brilliant actions George Custer ever directed."[65] He and Devin's units repulsed the Confederates, causing some four hundred casualties. Anderson and his commanders on the field were pleased that they had fought the Yankees to a draw, but Lee was less so with the loss of valuable veteran soldiers. On the other side, Sheridan was elated at the outcome. His cavalrymen had largely fought infantry troops and come out ahead. As Patchan writes, "The Battle of Crooked Run, Guard Hill or Second Front Royal proved to be a watershed occurrence in the Shenandoah Valley. Sheridan's Cavalry proved that they could stand toe-to-toe with the battle-hardened infantry of the Army of Northern Virginia."[66]

For the rest of the summer and fall of 1864, through a few false starts and stops, Sheridan and the Army of the Shenandoah pushed up the valley. In multiple battles, Custer impressed his commander with his calm actions in the chaos. When the leader of the Third Cavalry Division transferred to the Western Theater on 30 September, Sheridan promoted Custer, making him a major general and placing him at its head. He would lead the unit for the balance of the war. Custer's division contributed to the successful Shenandoah Valley Campaign, participating in the ravaging of the countryside that locals referred to as "the Burning." His command also defeated part of Early's force at the Battle of Tom's Brooks on 9 October, only ten days before the Federals' crushing victory at the Battle of Cedar Creek that drove the remnants of the Rebel army out of the valley.

With the end of that operation in late 1864 and early 1865, Sheridan, Custer, and their cavalry forces returned to the Army of the Potomac in February 1865 as it continued to lay siege to Petersburg, Virginia. After the Yankees overran the Confederate fieldworks later that spring, Custer and his division tracked down Lee's Army of Northern Virginia as it retreated toward Appomattox Court House, where Lee surrendered on 9 April 1865.[67]

By the time he received the first flag of truce that April day, Custer ranked as a popular hero among Federal officers. Some historians have noted that much of the Union's cavalry success, including Custer's, occurred after their Confederate counterparts had passed their combat peak. Even so, men like Custer were equal to whatever tasks came their way. As Jeffrey Wert writes, "A measure of a warrior is the ability to exploit enemy weaknesses, and in this, Custer had few peers. Combat fitted Custer as well as his distinctive uniform." He added that Custer may have been "the war's last knight. A soldier's duty merged with a personal quest for glory that made Custer a superb cavalry commander and a dashing, unmistakable hero."[68]

By the end of the war, Custer had gained Sheridan's full trust and ranked as one of "Little Phil's" favorite subordinates. In fact, the two men forged professional and personal ties during the war that extended through Custer's frontier career. Custer's dependability and fearlessness on the battlefield throughout 1864 and 1865 virtually guaranteed that he would deliver the results Sheridan demanded, and Sheridan rewarded Custer for it. After Grant and Lee concluded the surrender of Confederate forces, Sheridan reportedly paid twenty dollars for the oval-shaped pine table used in the negotiations. Sheridan gave the table to Custer as a gift for Libbie, telling her in an accompanying note that "there is scarcely an individual in our service who has contributed more to bring about this desirable result than your gallant husband."[69] At least twice in their years together on the Great Plains, Sheridan would be forced to rescue Custer from his own foolish human impulses that almost cost him his regimental command. At the same time, Sheridan continued to rely on Custer.

In the years since the war ended, the general public has remained aware of Custer even as the names of his equally prominent contemporaries have slipped into the historical mists. Men such as George Crook, Ranald Mackenzie, Wesley Merritt, and Nelson Miles served equally well during the war. They also, arguably, performed better and for longer periods on the Great Plains during the post-war Indian campaigns. Yet it is Custer's name that endures, undoubtedly due to his disaster on the bluffs above the Little Big Horn River. Some of the reasons why may be attributable to a belief in Custer's Luck, which became almost immediately apparent after the conflict's conclusion. In the spring of 1865, Custer was assigned command of a makeshift division in Texas created in response to the federal government's concern that Confederate troops might still be active there. During this period, he was roundly criticized for his ruthless disciplinary methods when dealing with the volunteer troops under his command who simply wanted to go home. These actions included lashings and even one enlisted man's execution for desertion.[70]

Historians generally agree that Custer performed strongly during the Civil War. Some, however, snipe at Custer for his perceived arrogance, an overboard desire for glory, and an uncaring attitude toward risking the lives of his troopers. Despite these claims, two factors kept Custer's personal immaturity under control during the hostilities. Initially, his senior officers would not have tolerated nonsensical personal behavior from a junior leader. By the time he had married Libbie, he was a general who remained closely wrapped under the high expectations of his superiors. The war continued to present such exciting challenges for Custer that he easily retained a close grip on his personal feelings.

Between 1863 and 1865, Custer had earned his plaudits on the field of battle and the media had quickly discovered that he made good copy. Newspaper acclaim boosted him in the esteem of his countrymen. Within the army, some of his peers scoffed at his actions, his reputation, or his flamboyant tendencies. More senior officers, including Grant and Sheridan, certainly overshadowed Custer. Yet his commanders realized that on the battlefield Custer delivered victory after victory.

Among the more supportive modern historians has been Gregory Urwin, whose 1983 book on Custer's Civil War career, *Custer Victorious*, remains one of the more persuasive accounts about that period of Custer's life. In an introduction for a later reprint, Urwin concluded that Custer was "one of the finest cavalry commanders to emerge from the Civil War, a quick-thinking tactician and inspiring leader who attracted the admiration and love of his officers and men. He outfought and outsmarted the pride of the Confederate cavalry while it was in its prime."[71] Sadly, as Urwin writes in his last line of *Custer Victorious*, "The worst years in the history of the United States and the best years of his young life were over."[72] Custer's celebrity status cemented, the challenge ahead for him was how to maintain that ranking for the rest of his career.

3 On the Central and Southern Plains

In the early months of 1866, Custer found himself at a personal crossroads. The previous December, he had turned twenty-six, which meant he was no longer truly young. Four years of war had left him drained and puzzled. Most members of the Army of the Potomac happily headed home to their loved ones and to resume their previous lives. That opportunity was impossible for Custer, however. His identity was bound up in his military service. As a cadet before the war, he had been a mere boy. As a general officer, he had earned praise and admiration for his battlefield skills, even if Texas proved an unpleasant interlude. What would he, as an adult, do next?

In September 1866, he had shown interest in politics when he joined Democratic president Andrew Johnson on his "Swing Around the Circle," his attempt to increase support for his policies toward the South. Radical Republicans heavily criticized Custer and, as soon as possible, he dropped out of Johnson's entourage. Custer toyed with two other possibilities in 1866. First, the Mexican government, in the midst of fighting French forces that had invaded and occupied the country starting in 1862, offered him sixteen-thousand-dollars-a-year to serve as its army's adjutant general. The financial offer tempted him, especially after General Ulysses S. Grant and Secretary of War Edwin M. Stanton assented. Secretary of State William H. Seward, on the other hand, fearful of offending the French government, rejected Custer's request.[1]

At another point, some New York moneymen wined and dined Custer, thrilled to be close to a genuine war hero. They suggested that he could build on his fame to amass personal wealth in railroads and mining. Such enticements left the former blacksmith's son from New Rumley in over his head and, at least partially, he turned away from that option. He remained an army officer, but also invested in a silver mine and other schemes.[2]

Continuing with the army was also problematic. The postwar force was almost an entity the now Captain Custer—having received a brevet, or honorary, promotion to major general of volunteers, not the Regular Army—had not known before. It no longer called on divisions and corps to fight. Smaller aggregations, such as the regiment and company, became the units of note.

Still, Custer's Luck seemingly held that summer. With the Civil War over, Congress passed the Army Act of 1866 on 28 July, revamping the Regular Army's structure and increasing its strength. Custer proved more fortunate than most of his Civil War peers when he received a promotion to lieutenant colonel and an appointment to the newly created Seventh United States Cavalry Regiment. As its second-in-command, he joined the new unit on the Kansas plains for the next few years. A lieutenant colonel's rank was still far below his former major general's standing, but at least he would still be called by his brevet title.

For much of the nineteenth century, the United States Army had faced constabulary duty on an ever-expanding western frontier. After the Civil War, that task grew even more daunting. "The close of the Civil War opened a new chapter in the westward movement and thus in the army's mission," historian Robert M. Utley notes. "Peace released unprecedented national energies, which set off explosive development of the frontier West as well as an explosive industrial expansion in the East." In the two decades after the conflict, a rush of migration brought four million people into the region. Soon, railroads spanned the continent, mining shafts yielded mineral riches, cattle consumed the grasslands, and towns and farms emerged all over the territory, fulfilling Americans' concepts of Manifest Destiny.[3]

The United States faced a significant problem before its westward expansionism closed. The government needed to figure out how to handle the country's still sizable American Indian populace, including the Cheyennes, Arapahoes, Lakotas, Kiowas, and Comanches. These populations were some of the most formidable Indian people in North America.[4] All had previously fought off the United States Army and all were growing more anxious as thousands of white settlers poured onto the Great Plains.

In the late 1860s, the army stood as the only force in the region with sufficient authority and power to control outbreaks of violence, no matter who initiated it. Not surprisingly for men largely drawn from the east, few of its personnel, from generals to privates, possessed deep knowledge of or insight into the indigenous people. They viewed Indians merely as savages who would murder a white person for no reason if given half a chance. It is also fanciful to suggest Indians held significant insights and understanding into white culture. In reality, many Indian assumptions about white Americans were equally unclear. Most found little to like about white culture, preferring instead their traditional ways of hunting buffalo and moving freely along the plains. They also understood little about white culture as an example from 1870 illustrates. An agent accompanying the Lakota delegations of Red Cloud and Spotted Tail on an Eastern swing overheard several of the delegates discussing the great number of whites they were seeing on their journey. "The astonished warriors could only reason that they were seeing the same people in each city," the agent recorded. "The people in Chicago had somehow followed them to Washington, Philadelphia, and then New York. The delegates were convinced that white men," he continued, "with their superior technology, had developed the means of moving whole cites, much like the Lakota themselves could move their tipi villages from one site to another."[5]

In reality, neither side truly grasped the others' motivation. In largely living apart, the two societies had little idea about the profound changes that would influence everyone in the coming decades. Neither white Americans nor Indians would continue living their respective traditional ways. That reality never occurred to George and Libbie Custer in their remaining time together. Libbie would live well into the twentieth century and experience many of the changes that already were approaching when, in October 1866, she and her husband arrived at Fort Riley, Kansas. Operating under the Department of the Missouri, which covered Kansas, Missouri, Colorado, and New Mexico, Fort Riley and the other Kansas forts watched over such trails as the Santa Fe Trail to New Mexico and the Smoky Hill Trail to Denver as well as the ongoing construction of the Union Pacific Railroad. The Department of the Missouri, based out of Fort Leavenworth, Kansas, was one of three sub-commands under the Military Division of the Missouri commanded by newly promoted Lieutenant General William T. Sherman and headquartered in Saint Louis, Missouri. Another familiar Civil War veteran, Major General Winfield Scott Hancock, who had commanded the Army of the Potomac's II Corps for much of the conflict, headed the department.

The soldiers in Custer's new regiment did not match the quality of the well-motivated cavalry volunteers in the Michigan Brigade who had enthusiastically enlisted to restore the nation. Few of the Seventh Cavalry horsemen, for example, matched another early enlistee in the regiment, former Private John Ryan. A second-generation Irish teenager, Ryan served three years in the Civil War with the Twenty-eighth Massachusetts Volunteer Infantry Regiment of the Irish Brigade and another seven months in the Sixty-first Massachusetts Volunteer Infantry Regiment during the siege of Petersburg, Virginia.[6] With his Civil War experience, his native-born status, and his unusual view of the army as a possible career, Ryan differed from the typical recruits of the Indian wars. Instead, the postbellum army attracted few high caliber recruits, making its enlisted component typically below mediocre.[7]

More recently, historian Paul L. Hedren has taken a somewhat different view of the post–Civil War army. He believes that the army and its senior officer corps were still planning for more conventional fighting in its doctrine, weaponry, and tactics. The army fared poorly in the late 1860s during Red Cloud's (the Bozeman Trail) War and had struggled against the Lakotas for three years along the Yellowstone River in the early 1870s. By 1876, however, the army was "in fact, rather capably led by a cadre of well-educated and well-seasoned officers," many of whom were veterans of the Civil War. The army was also better outfitted and well-armed.[8]

Custer did not immediately join the regiment at Fort Riley. Libbie and he first vacationed in Saint Louis, where Custer and the noted stage actor, Lawrence Barrett, began a lasting friendship. The Custers then headed for their new duty station, arriving in mid-October, but Custer's stay was cut short when he was recalled to Washington, D.C., in November to appear before an examining board related to his new commission. He remained there until just before Christmas. In the interim, Major John W. Davidson, the acting regimental commander, and other officers of the Second United States Cavalry had been forming the Seventh's companies.[9]

On 26 February 1867, Custer returned to the regiment. Its commander, Colonel Andrew J. Smith, an officer experienced in both Indian fighting and the Civil War, had departed to command the District of Upper Arkansas. From then on, the Seventh was viewed as Custer's unit, even though higher-ranking officers held command on paper. On the plains, his superiors were generally located hundreds of miles away. More often than not, he found himself independent of a senior officer's close watch. That freedom allowed him to make his own decisions, which permitted the boy within him to resurface. Soon, he led his new contingent on its first field campaign. Surely, Custer could control his own impulses.

In April 1867, General Hancock, accompanied by Custer and eight companies of the Seventh Cavalry, sought to meet with chiefs of the Southern Cheyennes, the Arapahoes, and the Apaches at Fort Larned, Kansas. The Indians were suspicious, however, fearful of a repeat of the infamous Sand Creek Massacre of 1864 that resulted in the deaths of 148 Southern Cheyennes. Hancock and Custer met with Indian leaders on 13 April and expected to meet again the next day, but the Indians slipped away overnight. An irritated Hancock ordered the Indian camp burned and sent the Seventh Cavalry in pursuit. The Indians scattered into smaller bands, making them more difficult to track. These groups began attacking whites along the Smoky Hill Road. Hancock's mission failed and, in the process, he managed to set off an Indian war on the southern plains.

The Seventh Cavalry spent six weeks in camp at Fort Hays, Kansas. During that time, the impatient Custer grew more irritable at his enforced inaction. Desertions ran high and many men abused alcohol, even in camp. In attempting to solve such issues, Custer returned to his strict Texas responses, which included lashings and public humiliation. Then, on 1 June 1867, Custer and six companies headed for the Platte River area in Nebraska where Indians, angry at Hancock's actions back in the spring, were again raiding. Traveling with Custer's command was the regiment's newly assigned junior major, Joel H. Elliott, who served with the Seventh Indiana Cavalry during the Civil War.

For this early June campaign, Custer received the directive to locate rampaging Indians who committed hostile acts between the Platte River to the north and the Smoky Hill River to the south.[10] His area of operations was vast, covering northeastern Colorado Territory, southwestern Nebraska, and north central and west central Kansas. Custer's orders seemed specific enough, but support for his cavalry force proved lacking. Once again, his new enemy, under a highly competent Oglala Lakota warrior named Pawnee Killer, refused to act like his former Confederate foes. They were not easy to find on the hot, dusty prairie. Whenever they were located, they seemed to magically disappear just as quickly. Indian fighting was new to Custer and his peers, who all remained in a learning mode.

During this period, the first of dozens of men deserted Custer's unit, a problem that only grew worse during the six-week operation. Desertions interfered with his regimental command and control. They led to further controversy for Custer and his officers after he undertook dramatic measures to deal with the issue.[11] By early July, the elusive Indians had embarrassed the Seventh Cavalry as more and more soldiers absconded. On 7 July, as he continued his patrols, ten men fled the column, five on horseback and five on foot. Custer immediately issued highly controversial orders to chase the men down and "bring the dead bodies of as many as could be overtaken back to camp."[12] Shots were exchanged and three men fell wounded. They were placed in a wagon and traveled with the command for about ten miles to the next camp. Custer directed Surgeon Isaac Coates, in the presence of the men, not to treat the deserters' wounds. At a later court-martial, Custer testified that he eventually allowed Coates to treat them, but not in view of the remaining enlisted troops.[13] Custer's drastic action defused the desertion problem for the campaign, which ended the following week, but his own difficulties arising from the shooting episode and his responses were only beginning.

In his early days as a brigadier general in June 1863, Custer also had much to learn quickly, but he soon mastered how to fight on that war's battlegrounds. During the conflict, he came to believe in his own uniqueness, his Custer's Luck, but on the Kansas plains replicating that success proved difficult. Indeed, for the first time in his military career, Custer found himself overmatched by recurring supply problems, weather, terrain, and his enemy. His own actions had resulted in the unnecessary deaths of his own men as well. Hundreds had abandoned his regiment. Worse, still, he would soon let personal desires overwhelm his professional responsibilities as a regimental commander in the face of the enemy.

Custer's campaign drew to a formal close when the Seventh Cavalry arrived at Fort Wallace in western Kansas on 13 July. The lengthy and tiring operation left his cavalrymen exhausted and with meager supplies. Custer then stumbled into a personal abyss that put his career in jeopardy. On that final day, the lieutenant colonel literally dumped regimental command off onto Major Elliott, an assignment that soon became permanent for the younger officer. No longer in charge, the boy within Custer now ran amuck.

After handing Elliott field command on 15 July 1867, with three officers and seventy-two enlisted men, Custer rode furiously from Fort Wallace to Fort Hays to obtain supplies, or at least that is what he claimed later. Less than sixty hours later, Custer and most of his detachment galloped into Fort Hays, a journey of approximately 150 miles.[14] Custer likely intended to travel on to visit his wife at Fort Riley as he and a smaller group pushed on to Fort Harker, arriving well after midnight on 19 July. Custer, riding hell-bent to visit his wife on the other side of Kansas, was more a smitten teenager than a disciplined army officer.

At Fort Harker, he submitted his report to the sleepy Colonel Smith and then took off for Fort Riley, but Smith recalled him immediately. Upon Custer's return, Smith had him arrested for leaving his command without permission, but he did allow Custer to join Libbie at Fort Riley while awaiting his trial. The subsequent court-martial charged Custer with "absence without leave from command" and "conduct to the prejudice of good order and military discipline."[15]

After a month-long trial, the court-martial board found Custer guilty of all the accusations. He was suspended from rank and command and forfeited his pay for a year. Following the verdict, the Custers incessantly whined that he received unfair treatment. Other officers thought otherwise. Grant, in his role as a reviewing officer for the proceedings, pointed out that the court, "in awarding so lenient a sentence for the offences [sic] of which the accused is found guilty, must have taken into account his previous service."[16] In reality, a lesser figure than Custer likely would have lost his army career entirely. In effect, his Civil War record and the pull of his friends among the senior command saved Custer. Just four years earlier, Lieutenant Granger had called Custer "one of the most perfect gentlemen" in the army. During that summer of 1867, that same "perfect gentleman" fled the scene.[17]

The whole episode remains controversial. Many students of Custer's life claim he was punished as a scapegoat for Hancock's own failures. Testimony from the court-martial indicates his actions were certainly blameworthy, but the charge that summer could be viewed as more a matter of legal semantics. Whether one judges Custer's sentence as too severe or too lenient, he clearly paid a high price for his self-centeredness.

Custer's experiences in 1867 taught him little. The Indians in Kansas had baffled him. The campaigning significantly differed from those during the Civil War. His own foolish mistakes put his career at risk. Yet, he found little personal blame in his actions. Instead, he viewed himself merely as a scapegoat. Few of his military peers supported that interpretation.

While many of his friends, including Major General Philip H. Sheridan, retained their admiration for Custer's military skills, he had also weakened himself in their eyes. After his court-martial, Sheridan wrote that Custer had "done many things which I do not approve of." He believed that although Custer had "held high command during the Rebellion," the lieutenant colonel had "found some difficulty in adapting himself to his altered position" after the conflict.[18] Custer would yet resurrect his legend on the plains, but little he did in 1867 enabled him to move in that direction.

Historians have offered different reasons for Custer's struggles that year. Robert Utley blames Custer for his own downfall. Campaigning and living on the plains so differed from the Civil War that Custer proved less capable in dealing with all the changes. "Both personally and professionally," Utley argues, "Custer's new world imposed new and hard terms not easily mastered." For Utley, Custer suffered from an identity crisis at the time that could have cost him his career.[19]

Louise Barnett believes Custer simply could not handle such a fall in rank and prestige in so short a period. "Far in the lesser venues of frontier duty," she writes, "he was not recognizable as the man he had been—the popular Civil War general." The move to the Great Plains seemed "to produce a change in character that supplanted the solicitous commander with an aloof and unfeeling martinet," Barnett states. Although his friends still admired him, for others, he had become "unappealingly self-absorbed."[20] Barnett's assessment of Custer is certainly telling. It is important to remember that Custer often had been his own worst enemy with his flawed decision-making, such as encouraging his fellow cadets to continue fighting at West Point or ordering his officers to shoot down deserters. In his worst moments, no unjust system tripped Custer up. He somehow always managed to do that to himself.

Despite the Custers' believing they had been victimized, an important friend largely stood by them. Sheridan let the Custers use his quarters at Fort Leavenworth for as long as they wished after the court-martial. They stayed the rest of the fall and winter, pleased, at least, to spend all their time together without having to worry about military demands and operations. When the troops began preparing for another campaigning season in the spring of 1868, apparently stirring George's leanings as a soldier, the Custers headed back to the Bacon house in Monroe where George spent time working on his memoirs and hunting and fishing. They also visited friends across Michigan and Ohio.[21]

Although Custer's court-martial disappointed Sheridan, he soon recovered. By the fall of 1868, Sheridan needed Custer once more to serve as his war horse. In early September, Colonel Alfred Sully led a failed campaign against the Southern Cheyennes and Arapahoes in Kansas. Later that month, some seven hundred Southern Cheyennes attacked a command of scouts under Major George A. Forsyth along the Arickaree Fork of the Republican River in eastern Colorado. Forsyth and his men held them off while taking refuge on a sandbar in the middle of the river until troops of the Tenth United States Cavalry rescued them. One officer and four scouts were killed in the ambush. Sheridan and Sherman knew that stronger measures were needed to punish the offending tribes.

After these disastrous operations, Sheridan persuaded President Johnson to allow Custer's return before he had fully served his year's sentence on his court-martial. His return, however, would bring another whole set of controversies with it. Early on the morning of 4 October 1868, Custer stepped off a special railroad car that had transported him to Ellsworth, Kansas, enroute to retake command of the Seventh Cavalry. When Sheridan and Custer met at Fort Harker, Sheridan reportedly said that he could "smoke a cigar in peace once more as Custer had never failed him."[22] Custer was the man for the unpleasant job Sheridan was handing him, no matter how nasty it may appear to many modern Americans. Violent clashes between white Americans and Indians were about to become more numerous and more bloody, especially for the Cheyennes and the Seventh Cavalry. Sheridan's plan for Custer's unit involved some new approaches, including elements of total war, campaigning during the winter, and the employment of converging columns.[23]

Three military forces were being organized that fall to hit the Indians in their winter camps that Sheridan and his officers believed lay on the Canadian and Washita rivers in Indian Territory (modern-day Oklahoma). From Fort Lyon in Colorado, Major Eugene A. Carr would move southeast. A second force under Major Andrew W. Evans would deploy from Fort Bascom, New Mexico Territory. They would act as what Utley terms "beaters" for the army's third column, marching southeast from Fort Dodge on the Arkansas River in Kansas.

Alfred Sully, as district commander for the Upper Arkansas, led this last force, but Sheridan intended to tag along. Eventually, Sheridan sent Sully back to his department headquarters and turned to Custer as field commander. On 21 November, Sheridan issued general directions to Custer. He ordered the column to "proceed south, in the direction of the Antelope Hills, thence towards the Washita River, the supposed winter seat of the hostile tribes; to destroy their village and ponies; to kill or hang all warriors, and bring back all women and children."[24] Otherwise, Sheridan showed his faith in the younger man, telling him that he would "rely in every thing upon you and shall send you on this expedition without giving you any orders leaving you to act entirely upon your own judgment."[25]

The Seventh Cavalry initially set out from a post known as Camp Supply on 21 November, but a blizzard slowed their progress. Early in the morning six days later, Custer outlined his plan of attack for his officers along the wintery countryside. The regiment followed a trail that a war party of young warriors made while returning home from raiding in the Smoky Hill country of Kansas that Major Elliott had located a few days before. Some of the approximately 150 men had come from the villages travelling with Southern Cheyenne leader Black Kettle.

The United States Army had attacked Black Kettle's people once before. Considered a significant peace chief, Black Kettle had received permission for his people to hunt along the banks of Sand Creek in Colorado in late November 1864. On 29 November, as Black Kettle met with local Indian agents, Colorado volunteers under Colonel John M. Chivington attacked the camp and massacred 148 Southern Cheyennes.[26] By 1868, Black Kettle's prestige had sagged among his people and his band numbered only fifty-one lodges tucked into a wind-protected alcove along the Washita River. While he still maneuvered to assure peace between the Cheyennes and the whites, his young warriors remained hopelessly dedicated to war and gaining prestige. As Utley describes Black Kettle's band, they "could not be characterized according to the white people's simplistic labels of 'peaceful' or 'hostile.'"[27] They were both, and many of the young warriors had joined in the raids on the Kansas settlements.

Now, almost four years after Sand Creek, on the morning of 27 November 1868, Custer divided his troops into four battalions as the column neared the end of the trail. He planned on surrounding the village and launching coordinated attacks from multiple directions. After setting their positions, a shot rang out and the troops charged. Within ten minutes, two of the battalions had entered the village, but a delay from two others left an opening on one side of the camp. Multiple still mobile Indians escaped through that gap, fled through the icy waters of the Washita, or hid in nearby ravines. Among those who did not make it out of the village were Black Kettle and his wife. While riding the same pony, the chief and his wife fell dead into the river after getting hit by random gunfire.[28] With the army continuing the assault, noncombatants sought to escape, and warriors kept up their resistance.

At one point, scout Ben Clark reported to Custer that men in one of the contingents were indiscriminately shooting women and children. Custer immediately ordered Clark to "ride out there and give the officer commanding my compliments and ask him to stop it. Take them to the village and put them in a big tipi and station a guard over them."[29] At another point, Elliott gathered up an eighteen-man detachment to chase fleeing Cheyennes. He and his men were never seen alive again.

Custer soon confronted hundreds of additional warriors who had come from nearby encampments. Once the aggressor, Custer now found himself on the defensive and an increasing number of warriors were milling about out of range. Amid the chaos, Custer faced a host of problems. At one point, Lieutenant James Bell, the regiment's quartermaster officer, drove his ammunition wagons through the Indians. Custer's larger, weakly defended supply train remained vulnerable on the army's back trail. Prior to making the attack, the Seventh's troopers had doffed their heavy winter garments despite the bitter cold. Approaching warriors drove off a guard force and seized the regiment's overcoats and haversacks. Additionally, the cavalrymen captured several prisoners and 875 ponies that he had no way of handling.

In this precarious position, Custer received word that Elliott's detachment disappeared while chasing after some refugees. Custer ordered a search for Elliott and his men, but they were not located. Custer then directed troopers to burn the village as several lines of skirmishers engaged the Cheyennes at a long distance, keeping the warriors at bay in the hills. The flames engulfed the possessions, food, and tepees of Black Kettle's people. Next, Custer ordered the execution of most of the captured ponies. His men found evidence of the raids in Kansas used later to justify the attack, including, as historian Jerome A. Greene notes, "unopened mail, photographs, and various household goods." Clark reported finding four white and three Indian scalps in the camp as well.[30]

Late in the afternoon, Custer formed his command into new columns to march down the valley toward the adjacent Indian encampments. He made no attempt to conceal his actions, which were meant as a bluff. The warriors, fearing Custer's intent to strike their villages, melted away to prepare a defense while their families fled. Custer marched until after dark. With the Cheyennes out of sight around 10:00 PM, he pulled in his skirmishers and the force headed back up its original trail. The next day, a squadron hurried ahead to the still intact supply train. By the next afternoon, Custer had reunited all his surviving troops.

Sheridan's orders to Custer had been explicit enough about how to deal with the followers of Black Kettle and the neighboring villages. He was to destroy their possessions and kill or hang the warriors and did so accordingly at the Washita. Even then, he acted quickly enough to prevent his Osage scouts and his troopers from killing non-combatants after being alerted to their violent outbursts.

Ever since Washita, however, Custer has been roundly criticized for its outcome. Ron Chernow states, for example, that "Custer and his cavalry obliterated an Indian village on the Washita River, wantonly murdering more than a hundred Southern Cheyenne, including women and children."[31] Custer did destroy the camp and the Cheyenne casualties were high, but Chernow fails to point out that Elliott had followed a trail that a 150-man war party of young warriors made when returning home after raiding in the Smoky Hill country of Kansas.[32]

According to researcher Richard Hardorff, the war parties had committed some seventy-eight specific acts of aggression in Kansas that had resulted in the deaths of 12 soldiers and 131 civilians, the rape of 15 women, and the capture of several children. They also burned "twelve farms, two stage buildings, a ranch, and three wagon trains and captured 735 horses and mules and 931 head of stock."[33]

Hardorff concluded that the Indian attacks had caused considerable embarrassment to Sheridan as well. Facing "political pressure and sharp criticism from special interest groups," Sheridan took an aggressive approach to his winter strategy.[34] Undoubtedly, he endured considerable complaining about the deaths of so many white men and women. In carrying out Sheridan's orders, Custer's troops may have matched the brutality of the raiders' own actions in Kansas that had angered Sheridan. The nature of war on the Great Plains in the late 1860s and 1870s meant that neither side was innocent.

Custer returned to the Washita battlefield with Sheridan in early December to ascertain what happened to Elliott's detachment. Searchers located the troopers, who the Cheyennes had cut off and killed not far from Black Kettle's campsite.[35] Elliott's body was first buried at Fort Cobb, eventually being reburied in the Fort Gibson National Cemetery in Oklahoma.[36] In one of the adjacent camps, the party also discovered the bodies of white prisoners, Clara Blinn and her two-year-old son Willie, both of whom had been captured in a raid on the Arkansas River on 8 October 1868.

Custer receives additional criticism for his perceived failure to order an adequate search for Elliott's squadron. Elliott and his men, however, had disappeared and been wiped out at some point during the fighting, but no one can pinpoint exactly when they met their fate. After the initial attack, Elliott dashed across the valley floor and onto the first bluffs, stationing himself on a knoll near Custer's headquarter site. When he spotted Cheyennes escaping through the cavalry lines, he rounded up the detachment, headed by Sergeant Major Walter Kennedy. As Elliott rode off, he reportedly yelled to Lieutenant Owen Hale, "Here goes for a brevet or a coffin."[37]

John Ryan also heard Elliott as he rode off. He recorded that "as soon as the Indians were overcome men were sent out to collect all the ponies they could find, and I, with five or six men of my company, was among the number." At that moment, "Major Elliott rode by with 18 men, trying to overtake those Indians who had broken through the lines. He sung out to me as he passed by," he continued, "'Sergeant, take those Indians prisoners,' referring to some squaws we were following. We did take some of them. We also captured the ponies they were driving, and it proved to be very fortunate for me and my squad that we did not go with Elliott." That moment was the last time Ryan and his companions saw horsemen under Elliott until two weeks later when they found their remains.[38]

Several theories exist about Custer's inability to aid Elliott. Custer remained in the dark about Elliott's whereabouts during the clash, but captured Cheyenne women confirmed that other camps existed farther downstream. Custer grasped that his easy victory may have been slipping away, causing him to order the burning of the village and sending skirmishers out to engage the Cheyennes at long distance.[39] Amid all of this action, Custer dispatched Captain Edward Myers' company to follow Elliott's troop. Myers claimed that he searched for two miles, but he likely proved less thorough. Custer later wrote that the ground within the lines that the counter attacking Indians held after the village's capture was "closely and carefully examined, . . . but with no success."[40] Lieutenant Edward S. Godfrey also reported that he "learned afterward that [Myers] did not go down the valley any distance else he would have discovered Elliott."[41] Custer presumably trusted his subordinate's word, leaving him to abandon further investigation.

According to a second theory, additional efforts at finding Elliott's detail would have put the entire regiment at risk. Custer, as the field commander, bore the responsibility for safeguarding his cavalrymen. By effectively leaving a comrade whose status at best remained unclear at the time, however, he may have sealed Elliott's doom. Conversely, if

Custer remained engaged with the encircling warriors, he could have lost an even greater number of soldiers beyond Elliott and his squad.

Other researchers blame Elliott himself for riding off on what Utley describes as "an independent glory-seeking expedition without orders or permission."[42] As the regiment's second-in-command, Elliott's responsibility was to remain close to his commander, prepared to step in if Custer were incapacitated. He failed to do so and, in turn, caused the deaths of his men and himself.

Other theories exist that discuss the long-term effects of Elliott's death and the so-called "Abandonment Controversy" on the Seventh Cavalry. Utley argues that Elliott's death would "haunt the Seventh Cavalry for eight years." He believes that moment at Washita likely darkened the "thoughts of more than one officer as the fateful events of June 25, 1876, unfolded along the Little Bighorn."[43] Utley's comment breaks the supposed controversy into two components. First, it claims that Elliott's death "haunted" the regiment; second, that the major's death still impacted Custer's relationship with his officers and the Seventh Cavalry's performance in 1876.

Understandably, Elliott's demise may have unnerved the Seventh's troopers on a stressful, dark night on the unlit bluffs above the Little Big Horn River. Colonel W. A. Graham, in his legendary work *The Custer Myth*, noted that on the night of 25 June, the besieged members of Reno's command did not know what had happened to Custer. Instead, many likely remembered the Elliott incident and believed that Custer had "found the Indians too strong and had gone to meet Terry, leaving them to fight it out as best they could."[44] Custer's defeat and death nearly eight years later at the Little Big Horn may be blamed on many factors, but Elliott's death at the Washita cannot be one of them.

Custer's return in the fall of 1868 and his muddied triumph at the Washita River brought him as much criticism as praise. In the battle's wake, Custer busied himself with military matters. He showed little interest in engaging the controversies surrounding whether Black Kettle and his people had been guilty of anything more than an inability to control their young men. In the ensuing months, Custer's so-called victory came under fire from multiple sources. Thomas Murphy, superintendent of Indian affairs, for instance, proclaimed to Nathaniel G. Taylor, commissioner of Indian affairs, that Black Kettle had been "one of the best and truest friends the whites have ever had, amongst the Indians of the Plains."[45] Black Kettle sought to maintain the peace between the races and did not deserve to die in combat against the army, Taylor claimed. Major Edward W. Wynkoop, former agent for the Southern Cheyennes and Arapahoes, also protested the Seventh Cavalry's actions. He resigned his post, comparing Custer's attack to Chivington's unprovoked butchery of Black Kettle's people along the banks of Sand Creek four years earlier.[46]

Custer, in his later memoirs, claimed he would have been criticized regardless of the outcome of that fall campaign. If Custer had failed in his mission, white settlers, especially those who were targets of Indian raids, would have denounced him for being "inefficient or lukewarm in the performance." If he succeeded, he believed that "a wail would rise up from the horrified humanitarians throughout the country, and we would be accused of attacking and killing friendly and defenseless Indians."[47]

Taylor, Murphy, and Wynkoop led the way in that criticism, which eventually included members of the United States Senate Committee on Indian Affairs as well as some eastern newspapers. Cherokee, Choctaw, and Creek representatives who supported the Southern Cheyennes called the Custer attack "a brutal massacre of friendly Indians" and demanded an investigation.[48] Sherman, mounting the army's defense, sought to blame Black Kettle. He argued that the Cheyenne leader may have been personally peaceful, but was unable or unwilling to prevent his young warriors from attacking white settlers. The debate lingered for months. Westerners voiced support for the army. Easterners largely lambasted the action.[49]

Despite civilian criticism and negative newspaper accounts related to Washita, Custer's own reputation was only modestly affected. For once, his larger than life personality remained secondary to the event itself. To most Americans, the western plains remained an untamed and mysterious land. The only people who had roamed that space, the Plains Indians, were considered unknowns, even being inappropriately dismissed as mere savages in an alien place. In that time, white peace advocates began a more generous uplifting view of indigenous people, but in late 1868 that was not yet the norm.

Today, Washita is often labeled as a massacre and cited as a sign of Custer's hatred of Indians and his desire to snuff out their way of life. Overlooked from that same period are his actions on the Staked Plains of Texas in 1869 as he continued efforts to bring the remaining Southern Cheyennes to bay. The number of Indians from the Southern Plains who surrendered in December 1868, and in January and February 1869 overwhelmed the capacities of Fort Cobb. Sheridan ordered the construction of a new larger facility, Fort Sill, to handle and care for the increased numbers of native people who turned themselves in to the army. In early March 1869, Custer with eleven companies of the Seventh Cavalry and ten companies of the Nineteenth Kansas Volunteer Cavalry set out to locate the Cheyennes. They went to force both their surrender and the release of two white women, Anna Belle Brewster Morgan and Sarah Catherine White, being held hostage. Within days, his command suffered considerably and he was forced to reduce his numbers. Some four hundred of his own weakened cavalrymen and all of the Kansas volunteers were sent back to Camp Inman, a supply depot near the Washita battlefield.[50]

By 15 March, with his men living on butchered mule meat, Custer came upon an extensive Cheyenne village under Medicine Arrows along Sweetwater Creek, just west of the Texas-Oklahoma border. Custer deployed his troops around the multiple camps as he rode forward to parley with the chiefs. In his memoir, Custer assured his readers that this dangerous move was well-intentioned and not foolhardy. "No one could be more thoroughly convinced of the treachery and bloodthirsty disposition of the Indian than I am," he wrote, "nor would I ever trust life in their hands except it was to their interest to preserve that life."[51] Ryan questioned his commander's wisdom. He later wrote that he thought it was a "very foolish thing to do, to ride right in among the Indians."[52]

For three days, Custer negotiated with the village leaders. Custer avoided firing a single shot upon the inhabitants at Sweetwater Creek during the meetings. At one point, Medicine Arrows emptied the ashes from his pipe onto Custer's boots, a gesture that purportedly ensured Custer's future bad luck. According to Cheyenne oral history, Custer's death at the Little Big Horn resulted from his breaking his promise not to engage the Cheyenne.

During these discussions, Custer ordered the seizure of several of the chiefs, holding them hostage. He promised their release, as well as the liberation of prisoners taken at Washita, once the Cheyennes agreed to surrender. As the negotiations dragged on, Custer issued an ultimatum. If Morgan and White were not released within twenty-four hours, he proclaimed, he would hang his hostages. His threat worked. The Cheyennes surrendered and they released Morgan and White.[53] Successfully completing his mission, Custer and the Seventh Cavalry began the long trek back to Camp Inman. Custer continued holding the Cheyenne leaders he took hostage and brought them back to the depot. Unlike his operation the previous fall, no fighting occurred in Texas that March.

After their return from the Staked Plains, Custer and the Seventh Cavalry remained at Fort Hays. In April and May 1869, the companies were split up and sent to Forts Leavenworth, Dodge, Harker, Hays, and Wallace in Kansas, and to Fort Lyon in southeastern Colorado. With the regimental headquarters remaining at Fort Hays, the Custers camped along its parade ground among the trees that spring and summer.[54] When the Seventh Cavalry resumed patrolling the plains in the spring of 1870, they all returned to Fort Hays. During that tour, the unit only occasionally experienced minor clashes with roaming bands of warriors more intent on stealing cattle than causing other mischief. For two years, the once aggressive "Boy General" had to bide his time. Libbie and he spent their summers leisurely in their grassy camp at Fort Hays. When winter's cold weather forced them to retreat indoors, they lounged around at Fort Leavenworth, dominating the post's social scene.

During this period, Colonel Smith, the nominal commander of the Seventh Cavalry, retired from the army to become postmaster in Saint Louis. The ambitious Custer turned to Sheridan to garner support for a promotion to colonel and command of the regiment. On 2 March 1869, Sheridan wrote to him that he would push Custer's "claims on the subject of promotion as soon as I get to Washington, and, if anything can be done, you may rely on me to look out for your interests."[55]

Sheridan may have tried his best for Custer, but, in the end, the army's strict seniority system ruled. In that era, an individual's date of rank governed officer promotions. Numerous lieutenant colonels ranked ahead of Custer, now twenty-nine years old. He would have to wait for his own elevation to colonel. Instead, Colonel Samuel D. Sturgis replaced Smith. A West Point graduate of the class of 1846, Sturgis, the namesake of the Black Hills town, had fought in the United States-Mexican War, antebellum Indian wars, and the Civil War. Early in the rebellion, Sturgis fought well, eventually receiving a promotion to brigadier general of volunteers. In June 1864, however, he unsuccessfully led a combined cavalry and infantry force against troops under Confederate general Nathan Bedford Forrest at the Battle of Brice's Crossroads in Mississippi. His stinging defeat essentially ended his Civil War command. Still, he remained an officer with the volunteer forces until March 1865 when he reverted to lieutenant colonel in the Sixth United States Cavalry with the Regular Army. Although Sheridan failed in making Custer a colonel, he kept Sturgis largely on detached duty until 1876. Thus, Custer retained field command of the Seventh Cavalry.

For the next two years, Custer avoided getting ensnared in controversy, at least publicly. In the summers of 1869 and 1870, when not at Fort Hays, the Custers experienced the social life at Fort Leavenworth or returned home to Monroe. George also spent time in New York hoping, without success, to improve the couple's financial situation.

Some historians, including Utley and T. J. Stiles, have questioned if the Custers endured marital problems during this period. Some of the Custers' personal letters raise tantalizing hints, particularly about George. Cheyenne oral history suggests Custer engaged in a sexual relationship with Monahsetah, one of the Washita hostages. Captain Frederick W. Benteen contributed broadly to such beliefs. Despite much discussion and wide interpretation, English author Peter Harrison in his biography, *Monahsetah*, could not answer whether Custer engaged in such a relationship, including the possibility that Monahsetah bore his child. Harrison left it up to his readers to decide the issues for themselves.[56] Utley points out that from January to March 1869, Monahsetah remained Custer's prisoner in the field, after having given birth. According to Cheyenne accounts, she may have become pregnant in that time and bore another child later that year. It has been suggested that Custer fathered the child, but only conjecture supports this claim.

Some writers theorize that Libbie herself may have wandered in her feelings as well. Benteen claimed that George's decision to abandon his command in Kansas in 1867 may have been due to Libbie's reported feelings for one of his subordinates, Lieutenant Thomas B. Weir. Many have questioned the truth behind this possibility. Reportedly, Weir remained "a close and trusted confidant" of Libbie's after George's demise.[57] It seems highly unlikely that Libbie was ever truly guilty of a wandering eye, even if that cannot be said about George.

A long-rumored transfer for the regiment proved true in March 1871. Militarily, the great war between the states had been over for six years. Politically, however, a more lengthy period of healing remained in its beginning stages, the effects of which the country feels even today. The United States victory in the conflict compelled the vanquished southern states to remain in the Union, but controversy reigned over how to readmit them. The twelve-year period from 1865 to 1877 consisted of the process of readmittance that became known as Reconstruction. National politics ensured that the process would be anything but easy. Indeed, the period was marked by frequent outbreaks of violence that required dispatching army units to southern states to maintain order.[58]

Inherent in the problems was a complex mix of racial, political, economic, and financial issues, none of which had seemed to concern the Seventh Cavalry, which for five years had sought to maintain peace on the Southern Plains. Between 1868 and 1871, the South experienced, as historian Eric Foner puts it, a "wave of counterrevolutionary terror."[59] So in 1871, the regiment's companies were scattered across the region. Custer took up the regiment's headquarters in Elizabethtown, Kentucky, about forty miles south of Louisville. For the next two years, he would enjoy routine duty and would both entertain and be entertained by others. At one point, he took leave for seven months to dabble in investments, hobnob with the rich and famous, and discuss politics, largely to no personal advantage.[60]

On 3 September 1871, Custer reported to his unit in Louisville before moving on to their post in Elizabethtown. Kentucky remained fairly peaceful during his tour of duty there.[61] Even while stationed in the South for the next two years, however, Custer never fully got away from the Great Plains. His status as a prominent figure of the West only grew.

George Custer's father, Emanuel, first settled in Ohio while training with his uncle to become a blacksmith. Little Bighorn Battlefield National Monument, National Park Service

Custer's mother, Maria, was the daughter of a local tavern owner in New Rumley, Ohio. She and Emanuel married after both of their first spouses died in the 1830s. Little Bighorn Battlefield National Monument, National Park Service

(opposite) *Not the most disciplined cadet, Custer nevertheless made his way through the rigorous curriculum at the United States Military Academy at West Point, New York, graduating in 1861.* Little Bighorn Battlefield National Monument, National Park Service

Major General Philip H. Sheridan (standing at left) and his cavalry officers, (left to right) Wesley Merritt, George Crook, James William Forsyth, and Custer, helped break the Confederate forces in Virginia in 1864 and 1865. Library of Congress

(opposite) *Custer, in his major general uniform, posed with his wife Elizabeth Bacon ("Libbie") Custer and younger brother Thomas W. Custer in spring 1865.* Library of Congress

Custer became renowned for his elaborate uniforms, such as this winter campaign uniform he wore in February 1868. Little Bighorn Battlefield National Monument, National Park Service

After the Battle of the Washita, Custer and his units held numerous Southern Cheyenne women and children prisoner, bringing them back to either Fort Hays or Dodge that winter. Little Bighorn Battlefield National Monument, National Park Service

The death of Major Joel H. Elliott, pictured here in 1867, sparked controversy for Custer as many military critics and reporters questioned why he limited the search for Elliott's detachment at the Washita. Sandy Barnard Collection

Custer's expedition into the Black Hills in 1874 included thousands of soldiers, scouts, and civilians who explored much of the region for the first time. South Dakota State Historical Society

During the Black Hills excursion, Custer and a small hunting party counted a grizzly bear as one of its prizes. South Dakota State Historical Society

(opposite) *Despite being remembered for his flowing blond locks, Custer had cut his hair short prior to the Montana Campaign in 1876.* Little Bighorn Battlefield National Monument, National Park Service

After the Battle of the Little Big Horn, Major Marcus A. Reno became a scapegoat for Custer's death. Little Bighorn Battlefield National Monument, National Park Service

Mark Kellogg was the only reporter to join Custer's column for the Montana Campaign. His initial notes provided the basis for early newspaper accounts. Sandy Barnard Collection

Libbie Custer, pictured here around 1875, assisted officers at Fort Abraham Lincoln in informing families at the post of the soldiers' fates in Montana a year later. Sandy Barnard Collection

Just five years after the Little Big Horn battle, the War Department erected a granite monument to the Seventh United States Cavalry on the site. Nine years later, the army placed white marble headstones marking where the men of Custer's command fell. Library of Congress

In 1910, Libbie Custer, who spent most of her life fighting to protect her husband's legacy, joined President William Howard Taft in Monroe, Michigan, to unveil the city's monument to the fallen lieutenant colonel. Little Bighorn Battlefield National Monument, National Park Service

After Custer's demise, numerous depictions, such as this dramatic portrayal from Pawnee Bill's Historic Wild West show in 1905, contributed to the myths surrounding his death. Library of Congress

4 On the Northern Great Plains

As the Seventh United States Cavalry was spread throughout the South, General Philip H. Sheridan invited George Custer to accompany him on a most pleasant assignment in January 1872. Sheridan planned a buffalo hunt for Grand Duke Alexei ("Alexis") Alexandrovich of Russia, the son of its Czar Alexander II, and his royal party as they toured North America. Sponsored by the United States government, the party acted as what writer T. J. Stiles calls a "kind of bison-killing diplomacy."[1] Additionally, Sicangu Lakota chief Spotted Tail and about one hundred of his men exhibited their buffalo hunting methods and put on a Sicangu war dance. The entire event proved memorable for all of its participants.[2]

Custer and the grand duke quickly became friends. In part thanks to Custer's affable personality and hunting skills, the buffalo diplomacy succeeded well beyond what the administration of President Ulysses S. Grant had hoped. After a few days hunting, Custer returned to the regiment's headquarters in Elizabethtown, Kentucky. His new Russian royal buddy soon followed and they met at Mammoth Cave. With Libbie joining the two men, they eventually traveled together to New Orleans where Alexis went aboard a Russian ship for the long journey back to his homeland. Four years later, Libbie received a letter of condolence from one of his aides. "About your heroic husband, the late General Custer," the letter read, "the Grand Duke speaks always in terms of the highest esteem and admiration, and the news of your sorrows afflicted him so much, that he could not resist the wish to express his sincere regrets."[3] Custer's little adventure with the Grand Duke saw him avoid any controversy. More important, it solidified his standing as a man of the West and a great hunter. It certainly did not hurt his reputation that William F. ("Buffalo Bill") Cody accompanied the group.

In the first quarter of 1873, Custer had slightly more than three years left to live. Between the entirety of his service during the Civil War and his eight years of military service since then, his life already stood as unique for a man of his times. It is likely that if he had died at that time few Americans today would remember him. Even Washita, controversial as it is today, would likely appear merely as a brief stain against his record. Custer would be no historical symbol or myth. The events that lifted him up to such a state—the Yellowstone Expedition of 1873, the Black Hills Expedition of 1874, and, of course, the Battle of the Little Big Horn—all occurred during his last three years.

After returning from hunting in Nebraska, Custer turned to yet another personal challenge. Already a successful army officer and western hunter, he now aspired to become a writer. According to Stiles, Custer "knew that he embodied the spirit of adventure in American culture—the daring soldier, the intrepid frontiersman. He wanted to be a public intellectual as well."[4] Between 1867 and 1875, he wrote, under the pseudonym "Nomad," fifteen letters published in a magazine called *Turf, Field and Farm*. At the same time, a new, wider-reaching publication, *Galaxy*, produced a personal serial starting in 1872 about his western career beginning with the Hancock Expedition of 1867 and the Indian wars of Kansas.[5] Its various installments were united under the continuing title of "My Life on the Plains." While readers both criticized and praised his efforts, considering his amateur status as a writer, he clearly enjoyed at least modest success. Custer, too, may have had the last laugh over his nineteenth century critics. Recognizing the popularity of his articles, the magazine's publisher, Sheldon and Company, gathered and published them as his popular memoir *My Life on the Plains* in 1874. It remains in print, while the words and works of many of his contemporary detractors have been lost to history.

After serving occupation duty for two years, Custer and the Seventh Cavalry learned in February 1873 that ten of the twelve companies would again take the field in the West. With new railroad surveys planned for the region, the army needed additional units back on the Northern Great Plains and the War Department reassigned the Seventh Cavalry from the Department of the South to the Department of Dakota. On 1 March 1873, the companies began their long marches to Fort Rice in Dakota Territory, first stopping in Yankton to wait out the winter weather. While waiting, the Custer tyrant of Texas resurfaced when he started implementing what Lieutenant Charles W. Larned called "ceaseless and unnecessary labor."[6] These actions initiated a growing mistrust among Custer's subordinates.

On 7 May, the Seventh Cavalry rode out of Yankton on a four hundred-mile trek to Fort Rice, reaching the far bank of the Missouri River a month later. Steamboats then ferried the soldiers and their horses to their temporary home. With no suitable lodging available, the Custers said their good-byes and Libbie headed for Monroe, Michigan, once again. Custer and the Seventh Cavalry stayed at Fort Rice while waiting for the army to complete their permanent station in central Dakota Territory, Fort Abraham Lincoln.

As the men of the Seventh Cavalry returned to the plains, the government was aiding the reach of the western railroads. Since the early 1850s, American politicians had longed to build a railroad across the northern tier of states and territories from Minnesota to Washington. In early fall 1871, an expedition surveyed some six hundred miles for a possible route for the Northern Pacific Railroad. Beginning on 15 July 1872, a second survey, commanded by Colonel David S. Stanley and accompanied by chief surveyor Thomas Rosser and his crew, extended its work even while skirmishing with American Indians.[7] A separate party from Fort Ellis, near

Bozeman, Montana Territory, had encountered a large contingent of Lakota warriors on 14 August 1872 at Pryor's Fork and ended its survey early.

The third Yellowstone Expedition, planned for the summer of 1873, would be the largest. By early that June, the Northern Pacific Railroad had been extended 450 miles across Minnesota and Dakota Territory, reaching the Missouri River at Bismarck. This upcoming survey would chart a possible route across western Dakota and Montana territories. The region was a vast remote area inhabited mainly by Lakotas and Northern Cheyennes, who all too often proved hostile to trespassers. The 1868 Treaty of Fort Laramie guaranteed a vast swatch in the two territories for the exclusive use of the two groups, but the nation's compulsion to push deeper into the West threatened their hold on their lands. Sheridan authorized a large military force to protect the surveyors under Rosser, one of Custer's best friends at West Point and a Confederate foe during the Civil War. Once again, Colonel Stanley would command the military's protective force.

Custer took ten companies when the Yellowstone Expedition set out from Fort Rice on 20 June 1873. Major Marcus A. Reno commanded the final two companies, which escorted another surveying crew marking the boundary between the United States and Canada that summer. Nineteen companies of infantry, plus large numbers of scouts, herders, and other civilians, numbering some fifteen hundred men in all, accompanied Custer's expedition.[8] As the huge column lumbered forth, Custer commanded his regiment, but remained under the direct supervision of Stanley. Clearly, the two men, who had disagreed over military matters earlier, would clash, which was not long in coming. Petty annoyances soon mushroomed into major catastrophes. At one point on 7 July 1873, Custer, the junior officer, refused to salute Stanley, who had him arrested and directed him to ride at the end of the lengthy column. Onlookers seemed to favor Custer, although they did not appreciate his disrespect of a superior officer.

Rosser intervened to gain Custer's freedom. Stanley and Custer managed to avoid further quarrels after the former allowed Custer to assume a scout's role, taking on the responsibility of blazing paths for Rosser and his crew. In mid-July, Stanley went on a three-day drinking binge. Custer may have contemplated assuming command of the expedition, but fortunately for his future never did.[9] In the end, as historian Robert M. Utley succinctly summarizes, the rows between the two officers were "largely a war of trivia but was rooted in Stanley's drinking and Custer's desire for freedom from supervision."[10] Utley further notes that from that point on leadership more often fell to Custer as Stanley continued to drink.

Custer's return to the Great Plains in 1873 was not without personal perils, as historian Louise Barnett outlines. Earlier, she notes, his personal and professional problems extended from his difficulty in adjusting to "a diminished career" after the Civil War. This time, however, she blamed his issues on "his lack of judgment in dealing with subordinates."[11] He often argued with his juniors and accompanying civilians.

Although Custer needlessly clashed with Stanley as well, such moments largely remained hidden away from the public. Still, their problems were prominent enough to cause their overall commander, Colonel Samuel D. Sturgis, to intervene, but Sturgis took no steps to end Custer's tyranny. At the same time, Custer bypassed his department head, Brigadier General Alfred H. Terry, on occasion to communicate directly with the latter's own superiors at the War Department. All in all, as Larned wrote, Custer was becoming "utterly detested by every line officer of the command . . . by his selfish, capricious, arbitrary and unjust conduct."[12] Stiles places less favor on Larned's complaints, pointing out that "Larned's remarks draw attention because he mastered the art of complaining." However, Larned outlined his view that army presonnel concluded Custer was merely pretentious and a self-promoting pest.[13]

In hindsight, one can judge the ineffectiveness of Custer's approach. On Civil War battlefields, Custer performed with distinction. Early in the conflict, he served on the staffs of highly competent generals, whom he watched and tried to learn from. Yet, Custer missed out on one important aspect in an officer's career development during the war—a lack of experience as a small unit commander. At first glance, that omission should not have so negatively influenced his efforts on the plains, but clearly the Custer of the late 1860s and early to mid-1870s, serving as a regimental commander in Kansas and in Dakota Territory, lacked an intuitive sense for being an effective peacetime commander. He seemed oblivious to how his own self-destructive behaviors undermined his standing in the eyes of his men and his superiors. The events along the Yellowstone allowed the worst side of Custer to resurface.

More than likely, Custer avoided career-ending censure for his frequent failures to handle people well because his superiors were generally located far away. Perhaps, too, he survived his boorishness because of his earlier successes on the battlefield. Up to that point in 1873, Custer had been a winner. As long as Custer retained that mystique, Sheridan, for one, remained a staunch protector. More often, Sheridan acted as a father figure rather than as a military superior, always pardoning Custer for his sins. He apparently always expected the younger man to deliver on his promises when caught in a fight. If Sheridan had seen the need to rein Custer in now and again, history might have turned out differently, but that was not the case.

During the expedition, in early August, Custer's own freedom from Stanley's supervision led to collisions with the Lakotas. The column required periodic resupply by steamboats. After one such rendezvous, Custer erected a fortified supply depot dubbed Stanley's Stockade. He left two companies of the Seventh Cavalry and one infantry company under Captain Frederick W. Benteen to protect the storehouse. Meanwhile, Custer, with about ninety other men in two companies, moved deeper into the Yellowstone Valley, known to be the home of Lakotas under Sitting Bull who lived in unceded territory adjacent to the Great Sioux Reservation in Dakota Territory.

On 4 August, about a half dozen Lakota warriors sought to stampede the horses of the two companies near the mouth of the Tongue River. Custer's small command of twenty men remounted and chased what was clearly a decoy force. A larger Lakota contingent almost captured Custer and his orderly, but they successfully rejoined the other eighteen men. Custer's troops slowly retreated to a timber line and held some three hundred fighters at a distance for a couple of hours. Soon, more United States soldiers arrived, forcing the Lakotas to yield the field. Custer's small party suffered only one man wounded, but the regimental veterinarian, Dr. John Holsinger, the sutler, Augustus Baliran, and Private John H. Ball were killed.

Usually critical of Custer, Stiles praises him for the successful action that day. Although he was "surprised, outnumbered, [and] isolated in the enemy's country, Custer handled his force with discretion and skill." Using the knowledge he had developed from his studies and mustering "all his old tactical instincts," Custer, according to Stiles, had "correctly read an ambush, kept his troops well in hand, maximized his firepower, and seized just the right moment to break the stalemate."[14]

Custer would have one more encounter with the Lakotas that month. On 8 August, with Stanley's permission, Custer launched a night pursuit of what he expected was the village from which his attackers had come four days earlier. By 10 August, Custer's eight companies followed the Indians' trail along the north side of the Yellowstone River to a point some three miles below the mouth of the Bighorn River. The

Lakotas had successfully crossed the deep, fast-flowing Yellowstone, but Custer's soldiers could not.

Early the next morning, Lakota warriors began firing on Custer's troops from the south bank. Other Lakotas crossed the river above and below the cavalry's campsite and advanced on their position. Once again, Custer responded without hesitation, successfully maneuvering his troops to force the Lakotas to retreat. He posted sharpshooters to face the threat from across the river and dispatched two companies apiece up and down the valley under captains Verling K. Hart and Thomas H. French respectively. To the west, Hart dispatched Lieutenant Charles Braden with twenty men to guard a bench land rising from the valley. Almost immediately, Braden's troops faced an onslaught of about two hundred warriors. Four times Braden's skirmishers repulsed their enemy. Braden was badly wounded in the action when a bullet shattered his leg.

To the east, French's squadron also blunted the attack. Custer, meanwhile, had the rest of the regiment mounted and ready for action in both directions. As the two bodies of cavalry charged, the Lakotas began fleeing. With Stanley's arrival, the artillery contingent fired their Rodman guns into the remaining Lakota positions. The battle along the Yellowstone was over. Praising Custer, Utley writes that he "had handled his command with calm deliberation and sound tactical instinct."[15] Stiles believes these clashes enhanced Custer's professional standing and provided "a counterweight to his terrible reputation within the military." He had reminded his friends and detractors alike that "whatever his institutional failings, he could still fight."[16] Although his victories were considerably minor fights, Custer was commended for successfully repulsing the redoubtable Lakota warriors of Sitting Bull, proving anew that he could be a highly capable military officer in a fight.

Custer and the Seventh Cavalry received an enthusiastic welcome when they returned from the trek into Montana

Territory. Their new duty station, Fort Abraham Lincoln, across the Missouri River from Bismarck, was now ready for occupation. Once again, Custer found himself on a peak in his life. He had avoided any actions that would have further undermined his reputation during the survey and served capably while protecting Rosser's surveyors and his largely civilian crew preparing the railroad's way across the Northern Great Plains. With his victories against the Lakotas, his standing as an Indian fighter now matched his reputation as a Civil War hero. As the head of the Seventh Cavalry, he also held sway as the commander of a new fort of combined cavalry and infantry. He had six companies stationed with him. Four more under Major Joseph G. Tilford were about twenty-five miles down the Missouri River at Fort Rice. The final two under Major Reno were stationed at Fort Totten, near Devil's Lake in Dakota Territory.

Soon after arriving at the new base, Custer found himself embroiled in a new controversy that involved Colonel William B. Hazen, now commander of Fort Buford, the northern most fort along the Missouri River. Custer and Hazen previously clashed at West Point and then after the Washita when Hazen commanded Fort Cobb in Indian Territory. Custer publicly supported the Northern Pacific Railroad, funded by the most renowned private bank in the United States, Jay Cooke and Associates, which was now entangled in financial difficulties. The federal government allowed railroads to control thousands of acres of public lands that they could sell to individuals or companies for massive profit. To realize such revenue, the railroad's administrators promoted the Dakota plains as a vast fruitful garden-to-be.

Hazen, essentially banished to far away Fort Buford, thought differently, writing that the railroad lands were worthless. He dismissed the region as an arid wasteland in summer and a frozen lake in winter. Custer stepped up to defend the Northern Pacific's investments with an article in the 17 April 1874 issue of the *Minneapolis Tribune*, which incensed Hazen. He struck back in his own writings. Perhaps of most significance was his privately published pamphlet, "Some Corrections of '*My Life on the Plains*'," which, among other statements, criticized Custer's account of the Washita.

In the end, the Custers continued to benefit from their close friendship with the railroad. Today, their acceptance of multiple perks likely would be seen as a conflict of interest, but that was not the case in the Gilded Age. Within the ethics of his time, Custer served the interests of the Northern Pacific Railroad, which army leaders also believed supported their best interests as well.[17] As Custer settled in at Fort Abraham Lincoln, however, the Panic of 1873 began on 18 September, dropping the United States into one of its worst economic depressions. No more work on the Northern Pacific Railroad would occur for some ten years. According to historian M. John Lubetkin, the Panic of 1873 lasted about five years and was second only to the Great Depression of the late 1920s and 1930s in its economic damage.[18]

In some respects, the country's financial setback may have had as much impact on Custer and the Lakotas as any other factor that brought them together in their violent clash nearly three years later along the Little Big Horn River in Montana Territory. According to the 1870 census, the total population of American settlers living in the 975-mile area between Duluth, Minnesota, and Bozeman, Montana Territory, numbered about twenty-five hundred people. They were almost entirely of European descent. The majority of them were soldiers. The area also remained home to tens of thousands of American Indians, most of whom lived west of the Missouri River, although they did not appear in the census. In proposing to raise millions of dollars to build the Northern Pacific Railroad through this uncharted territory, Jay Cooke and his business associates violated one of the basic tenets of railroad construction: to connect existing communities or largely populated regions.[19] Dakota and Montana territories offered no such possibilities.

For six or seven months after his return from the Yellowstone region, Custer largely passed his time at Fort Abraham Lincoln with his wife and members of his regiment. On occasion, his investment in the Stevens Mine in Colorado resurfaced, but it proved unsuccessful for the couple. As Stiles observes, "Undercapitalized, undermanaged, and oversold, its very purpose in question, Custer's mine staggered on, just barely alive."[20] At the same time, political and military leaders reviewed the clashes between whites and Indians on the northern plains and concluded that the government needed a stronger presence in the Black Hills of Dakota Territory, despite the risk that it might stir up ill feelings with the Lakotas.

Many modern writers divide the history of the Black Hills into two parts, before and after Custer's expedition of 1874. Historian Max E. Gilbert notes, however, that there was a "clear and continuous interest in the Black Hills and their mineral deposits dating as far back as 1743." He also believes that, by the 1850s, there was "a certainty that sooner or later gold would be discovered and that Custer would only play a role in destiny."[21]

Prior to the late-eighteenth century, all the Sioux bands lived in woodlands around the headwaters of the Mississippi River in modern-day Minnesota. During the middle of the century, they came out second best in their struggles against the Chippewas, who had the advantage of having received modern firearms from European traders. By 1775, only the Dakotas lived on those traditional lands. The other two major groups, including the Lakotas or "Teton Sioux," had relocated onto the Northern Great Plains. In time, the Lakotas' lives focused on following the migrations of the massive herds of bison that could provide for all of their needs. In adapting to their new homes, they increasingly relied on horses for transport, enabling them to become both dominant hunters and warriors.[22]

As their population migrated west at the time of the

American Revolution, the Lakotas, which consisted of seven sub-tribes—the Oglalas, Sans Arcs, Miniconjous, Brulés, Two Kettles, Blackfeet, and Hunkpapas, claimed a swath of land many times larger than even the largest colony. They took hold of portions of what became Minnesota, Iowa, Nebraska, North Dakota, and almost all of South Dakota. According to historian Edward Lazarus, they did not stay confined to those boundaries. Indeed, he writes that "Sioux raiders ventured as far north as Canada and as far south as Texas—anywhere the bison roamed."[23]

By 1814, the Lakotas, having expelled the Kiowas from their lands, claimed dominance over the Black Hills. Not long after, they pushed their plains empire into the Powder River country of northeastern Wyoming and southeastern Montana. These additions were significant as they created "a vast homeland for a people who cherished the land, lived off the land, and considered everything on or in the land in some way sacred."[24] After entering the region, the Lakotas grew in strength and overwhelmed the previous inhabitants, the Kiowas, Hidatsas, and Mandans. For about sixty years, the Lakotas remained supreme. Then, in the post–Civil War years, white expansion into the West resumed in earnest and the Black Hills were in the newcomers' path. For a generation, Lakota warriors would fight valiantly against these white incursions.

With the high likelihood of violent clashes between white settlers and Lakotas, Sheridan recommended that the army build a fort in the Black Hills to watch over the two groups, especially the Lakotas. Five years earlier, the Fort Laramie Treaty established the reservation in what is modern-day South Dakota, which included the Black Hills except for a portion in Wyoming. The treaty provided all that land for the Lakotas' exclusive use and barred white men from settling in or otherwise occupying the hills except for authorized government representatives. Sheridan argued that the army's presence in the Black Hills would make the Lakotas think twice about attacking any whites because of the threat of retaliation. As little was known about the heavily wooded, mountainous terrain that extended over the western portion of the Great Sioux Reservation, Sheridan decided to send a military expedition to explore the region. At first, he contemplated launching the effort from Fort Laramie in Wyoming Territory but realized that would more likely have led to clashes with the Lakotas and Northern Cheyennes. To avoid this possibility, Sheridan turned to Custer's regiment at Fort Abraham Lincoln to protect the excursion.[25]

On 2 July 1874, Custer's one-thousand-man column departed for the Black Hills seeking a site to locate a new fort. His military component was powerful, outfitted with ten of his own cavalry companies split between wing commanders Major Joseph Tilford and Major George A. ("Sandy") Forsyth, two companies of infantry, a battery of three Gatling guns, a Rodman cannon, and around one hundred wagons. Numerous civilians representing various sciences, including mapmakers, prospectors, geologists, and naturalists also traveled with the troops. Some sixty Arikara and Santee scouts joined the expedition as well.

For Custer, ever ready to do the army's bidding, the assignment came as he again pondered his own future. He remained an army officer, not so much due to its excitement, but more because he had yet to find success at doing anything else. His effort to find wealth in a gold mine failed and looking for opportunities to make a killing with investments merely saddled him with significant debts.[26]

His mission's main purpose may have been to scout for a suitable place to locate a fort, but some historians believe that Custer, enamored with somehow making his own fortune, saw an economic opportunity ahead. According to those researchers, Custer staffed his expedition with experts who might unlock the bounty that the Black Hills represented. Custer remained a military officer and not a successful entrepreneur, however, and it seems highly unlikely that he was capable of concocting such an elaborate scheme, at least on his own. He gained the assignment primarily because he was already stationed near the Black Hills and he had Sheridan's continued confidence and support. He did invite a number of scientists from such fields as geology, botany, and zoology. At first glance, this action might suggest he had ulterior motives beyond determining where to place an army fort, but those subjects also interested Custer himself.

Author Terry Mort notes that the most junior scientist, George Bird Grinnell, a Yale University paleontologist, also became the most renowned, although he was not one of Custer's invitees. Sheridan asked his personal friend and Grinnell's boss, Yale professor Othniel C. Marsh, to join. Marsh had to decline and sent Grinnell, the expedition's zoologist, in his place.[27]

Custer did invite geology professor Newton Winchell of the University of Minnesota. He had written to General Terry, the department commander, requesting such an addition to his staff. He reminded Terry that the hills were effectively new countryside and such an expert could prove highly useful.[28] Captain William H. Ludlow, chief engineer of Dakota Territory at the time and the expedition's engineering officer, also supported the appointment.

Four other civilians accompanied the column, including University of Minnesota botanist A. B. Donaldson and photographer William H. Illingworth. The final two men, miners Horatio Nelson Ross and William McKay, may have been the most obvious for a focus on gold. Who paid the civilians' way, according to Mort, remains unclear, but their presence and purpose were no secret.[29]

One key difference existed between Custer's experiences leading the surveys along the Yellowstone in 1873 and into the Black Hills in 1874. During the latter, Custer was fully in charge, which allowed him to play multiple roles on the trek. He acted as the commander as well as the chief scout, road maker, and hunter at times. These duties certainly overlapped and played to his strengths. He also had the responsibilities of locating one or more prospective places for the construction of a fort and safeguarding his command, including the civilians, his wagons, animals, and all manner of equipment. That second aspect meant avoiding combat with the Lakotas on their home turf. Thus, the mature Custer, not the "Boy General," needed to be in the saddle throughout the expedition's time in the field. Custer clearly was a man who enjoyed public praise. If the expedition were successful, the resultant publicity would match virtually any he had enjoyed previously, which gave him no room for failure. As Mort summarized, Custer was, "as usual, out to make a mark in history."[30]

As the group rode out of Fort Abraham Lincoln with several covers for its existence, Custer and his contingent thought about the Lakotas in the region. The strength of the excursion apparently caused the Lakotas to remain distant, even as they eyed its progress. According to John Ryan, now a first sergeant, "There was little or no danger to the powerful column, either real or apprehended. It started on a mysterious and romantic expedition, as if for a picnic, and as such it found the whole journey." Ryan also believed that its size so impressed the Lakotas that it "deterred the Indians from overt war that year."[31]

Feeling quite safe, members of the column paid special attention to the landscape. Ryan wrote that the soldiers and civilians "found a country of surpassing beauty and richness of soil, and the pasturage could not be finer. Timber was abundant and water both good and plentiful."[32]

The prairie approach to the Black Hills challenged the troops with what Mort calls its "checkerboard of vegetation."[33] The sun beat down, the wind blew constantly, and rain storms popped up frequently, knocking over tents and scattering animals and equipment. Mosquitoes and other insects often tormented men and beasts. Cottonwoods provided little in the way of burnable fuel for camp. By 18 July, the group reached the Belle Fourche River. The Black Hills lay ahead, offering a more hospitable environment. Of equal importance, Custer learned from a minor Hunkpapa Lakota leader named One Stab that no other Lakotas were in the vicinity. Custer's party essentially had the Black Hills to themselves.

On 30 July, the men encamped near French Creek in a valley south of Harney (now Black Elk) Peak. Four days later, Lieutenant James Calhoun recorded in his diary that the "prospectors accompanying the Expedition discovered gold this morning."[34] The grains of gold amounted to a mere handful. Still, it was enough to set off a rush into the Black Hills.

On 3 August, Custer moved south with five cavalry companies and dispatched scout Charley Reynolds on a ninety-mile solo ride to Fort Laramie with his report. Custer held back the news of the gold discovery until near the end of his dispatch and then downplayed its significance, pointing out how little had been found and likely knowing that the three newspaper reporters would not hold back the big news.[35] Mort describes Custer's message as "a classic example of diplomacy and self-promotion by modesty and indirection."[36] The newspapers did their job of playing up the story with large headlines.

Three days later, Custer and his men headed back to Fort Lincoln, having accomplished their mission. The next day, 7 August, Custer, Ludlow, Arikara scout Bloody Knife, and Private John Noonan saw a large bear, traditionally claimed to be a grizzly, on a nearby hillside as they approached the evening's camp site. Custer fired two shots with his Remington hunting rifle, followed by additional shots from his three companions. With the bear wounded, Bloody Knife cut its jugular vein to finish it off. Later, William Illingworth took a photograph of the four men with their prize, with Custer getting credit for the kill ever since.

Less than two weeks after first reporting gold in the hills to General Terry, Custer wrote him again addressing the official reason for the expedition. They found a perfect spot for building a new fort and he believed the country around the Black Hills was perfect for farming and stock raising. His positive commentary and the word of gold soon reached the public and scores of individuals laid plans to settle there. During the winter of 1874–1875, however, the Grant administration ordered the army to block white miners from trespassing on the Great Sioux Reservation in violation of the Fort Laramie Treaty, but their efforts became increasingly difficult.

By 30 August, after a torturous return trip, Custer's column reached Fort Abraham Lincoln. Early in September, George and Libbie went to visit Monroe, returning to the fort in November. Lakota and Cheyenne leaders frequently visited him that winter to express their complaints over dishonest Indian agents and the white miners invading the Black Hills. Libbie later claimed that her husband was adamant, after those winter meetings, that the government needed to keep its promises to the Indians. "He recognized a true nobility in the Indian character and respected their feelings of attachment for their land," she wrote. "There was a time after the Battle of Little Big Horn when I would not have said this, but as the years passed I have become convinced that the Indians were deeply wronged."[37]

The Black Hills decision was controversial even among white Americans. As writers Paul Horsted and Ernest Grafe note, Custer's Black Hills Expedition "resulted in a terrible loss for the Lakota people."[38] Many believe the Fort Laramie Treaty, specifically article twelve, barred all non-Indians from the area, but military brass rejected such restrictive interpretations. Instead, they contended that article twelve did not apply to government officials and the army. Although, as Horsted and Grafe observe, some army leaders argued that the treaty permitted military reconnaissance, it was difficult for them to defend Custer's exploration in 1874 considering that it included non-military personnel.[39] Historian Donald Jackson simply writes, "As carried out by Custer, the expedition was a treaty violation in spirit if not in fact."[40] Indeed, the clearest reason for the exploration, if not generally admitted publicly, was to search for gold rumored for years to be in the area's streams and hills. In such Dakota towns as Yankton and Bismarck, business leaders pressed Washington to allow white expansion into the hills, believing that it was natural and consistent with the country's westward movement.

At the time, many critics of Custer's expedition expected his presence in the Black Hills to cause a massive backlash from the Lakotas, but no such response came. Custer's column had no violent confrontations with them. His only casualties were two privates. One died from disease and the other by accident. Custer directly encountered Lakota people only in his peaceful meeting with One Stab. Another group of Lakotas stampeded some mules that the expedition soon recovered. Otherwise, the two sides left each other alone.

For the most part, Custer busied himself with exploring and hunting in the region's beautiful back country. Custer being Custer, he managed to involve himself in a bit of controversy that lingers to the present day due to the discovery of minor gold deposits. Custer downplayed it in his own dispatches, suggesting further study was needed. The mere hint of gold was enough to set off wild schemes and a large-scale invasion of the Black Hills. Custer made a handy scapegoat for the resultant gold fever that led to the Lakotas losing their sacred hills. After Custer's death and those of his 267 troops at the Little Big Horn two years later, numerous critics, even today, blame it all on Custer's role in invading the Black Hills. Many of these writers, however, overlook the facts that Custer's superiors had ordered him to explore the hills and that Lieutenant Colonel Richard I. Dodge of the Twenty-third United States Infantry Regiment led a follow up expedition there in 1875. Custer was certainly a player in the Black Hills debacle of the mid-1870s, but many others contributed to both his own downfall and the problems surrounding that country.

With gold fever now rampant among many white Americans in 1875, the government proved incapable of stopping miners from violating the Fort Laramie Treaty. The Grant administration advanced a simple solution, either buy the Black Hills for $6,000,000 or lease the land for $400,000 per year. The Lakotas, especially those under Sitting Bull and Crazy Horse who lived by more traditional customs on hunting grounds in unceded territory to the west of the reservation that had been promised to them in the treaty, had virtually no interest in selling their land for that amount, if at all. Tribal leaders, including Red Cloud and Spotted Tail, first heard about this suggestion when they met with government leaders in Washington, D.C., in June 1872. They returned to their agencies without a deal.

That September, a commission under United States Senator William B. Allison traveled to the Red Cloud Agency in Dakota Territory to propose the purchase again. By then, the Lakotas had broken down into various factions, including one led by Red Cloud, who was now considered merely a peace chief. The groups under Sitting Bull and Crazy Horse, the strongest opponents, made up approximately four hundred of the ten thousand Lakotas who attended. At one point, a contingent of the non-reservation Lakotas mounted a mock charge on the commission. After a couple days of negotiations, the Lakotas rejected the offer, to the government agents' frustration, believing the hills were worth more.[41]

With these failures, the issue of the Black Hills joined with the usual agency mismanagement problems to strengthen traditionalist Lakota leaders. By late fall, the Grant administration, fresh out of ideas to resolve the mess, moved toward a military solution. On 3 November 1875, Grant met with his new Secretary of Interior Zachariah Chandler, Secretary of

War William W. Belknap, Commissioner of Indian Affairs Edward Smith, the commander of the Department of the Platte Brigadier General George Crook, and Sheridan to discuss the issue. Not surprisingly, their focus on the Black Hills came from a white perspective on the potential economic value of the hills to the United States. The Washington bureaucrats paid little heed to the Lakotas' vastly different view. Instead, understanding the role that the traditionalist bands played in torpedoing the land sale, the president and his advisers decided that those Lakotas living on the unceded hunting grounds needed to be driven onto the reservation, despite the Fort Laramie Treaty.

On 6 December 1875, Chandler issued an order for the Lakotas in the unceded territory to report to the reservation by 31 January 1876. If they did not, the army would move against them to enforce the edict. The order was absurd. Even if those Lakotas had been inclined to follow it, the severe winter weather precluded such a move.[42]

At the same time in Dakota Territory, miners were laying out plans for their incursions into the Black Hills. Gold continued to beckon them, and the government seemed, if not powerless, highly disinclined to stop them. The outcome would prove tragic for many concerned.[43]

After the Seventh Cavalry returned to Fort Abraham Lincoln in 1874, a widespread debate began about whether Custer had truly discovered sufficient gold to merit large scale operations in the Black Hills. After Custer's death, the government controversially took control of the hills. Since then, much gold and other minerals have been mined from them. Ironically, Fort Meade, the post meant to maintain the army's presence in the region, was built near Bear Butte in the northern hills to protect the mining towns two years after Custer's death. The army never built a fort in the Black Hills proper.

In 1875, Custer, again without much thought of consequences, was setting himself up for a near-fall the following spring that could have ended his career and saved his life. By 2 June 1875, the Custers returned to Fort Abraham Lincoln, but faced a summer of relative inactivity. For one, the Lakotas, though angry at the invasion of their sacred hills, held back from sustained violence. Patrols by the Seventh Cavalry attempted to slow the onrush of prospectors into the Black Hills, but with only modest success.

At the same time, Custer was upset with the post sutler, Robert C. Seip, who had earlier raised prices to exorbitant levels. He complained to the War Department but Belknap backed Seip. The year before, Secretary of the Interior Columbus Delano revoked all Indian trading licenses for the department's posts on the Upper Missouri. To obtain a renewal, each trader had to turn to President Grant's brother, Orvil, who set demanding terms amounting to kickbacks. That scandal led to the ouster of Delano, but Belknap implemented a similar scheme for traders at the forts. Seip apparently paid a significant expenditure to maintain his monopoly at Fort Lincoln, a fact that Custer knew, and had increased his rates accordingly.

Meanwhile, Custer dabbled with what modern journalists would call "an informed source" for the *New York Herald*, an anti-Grant newspaper. Its publisher, James Gordon Bennett, Jr., had appointed his reporter Ralph Meeker to secretly investigate Belknap's corruption through inquiries in Bismarck and at the region's forts, using the alias J. D. Thompson. Only a handful of people reportedly knew Meeker's true identity, including Custer, *Bismarck Tribune* editor Clement A. Lounsberry, Bismarck postmistress Linda Slaughter, and newspaper reporter Mark H. Kellogg.[44] Meeker's investigative reporting led to a series of stories in the *Herald* in October and November that had repercussions the next year. As Utley observes, "Custer's complicity with Meeker and the *Herald* would form one of the strands in the rope that almost strangled him."[45]

In September 1875, free of military entanglements after

the expedition ended, Custer headed east to New York City. He again sought to raise money to support his investments, including the Stevens Mine. After Libbie later joined him, New York notables who never tired of meeting the celebrity general, Indian fighter, hunter, and writer frequently wined and dined the Custers. George often attended the theater, especially performances starring his friend, Lawrence P. Barrett, who had declined Custer's invitation to accompany the Black Hills expedition. He also dabbled in stock transactions that Stiles indicates were highly shady, if not illegal.[46] At the time, money was likely a significant problem for the couple.

Late in their stay, a promising opportunity arose, but Custer pushed it off to the future. The Redpath Lyceum Agency, one of the country's leading lecture bureaus, sought to sign him for a speaking tour that spring. Speaking five nights a week for four or five months, he could expect to make two hundred dollars a night, a sizeable sum for an army lieutenant colonel always desperate for a little more cash. Redpath wanted Custer to start that spring, but he desired more time to prepare so he delayed his tour. That decision would prove ironic, given his fate a few months later. As Utley observes, "Had not the Little Bighorn intervened, he might well have accumulated the modest fortune of which he so insistently dreamed."[47]

5

The Battle of the Little Big Horn

In the fall of 1875, President Ulysses S. Grant found himself in an awkward political, military, and humanitarian dilemma over the Black Hills. With the country still struggling economically under the weight of the Panic of 1873, he had approved sending George Custer and his Seventh United States Cavalry Regiment into the hills the previous year on an exploration mission that would determine how rich the region might be in gold deposits. Now, as miners overran the sacred lands of the Lakotas, the federal government needed to find a way to circumvent the earlier Fort Laramie Treaty of 1868 that bestowed ownership on the Lakotas. Facing miners invading the hills, the Lakotas felt compelled to take a stand.[1]

What followed was the order from the Department of the Interior calling for the so-called winter roamers, including those under Sitting Bull, and their Northern Cheyenne allies to join other bands on reservations in western Dakota Territory by the end of January 1876. Lakota attacks on the Crows, allies of the United States Army in the region, were cited partly to justify the order, but seizure of the Black Hills was the true purpose. On 1 February, the Interior Department dutifully notified the War Department that these traditionalist bands had failed to follow the instructions. It supplied a legal pretext for the planned military campaign, fueled by greed and disregard for the rights of American Indians.

Lieutenant General Philip H. Sheridan, overseeing the plans for the army, envisioned hitting the camps in these traditional hunting grounds from multiple directions, effectively repeating his successful winter strategy on the southern plains in 1868. The 1876 campaign, which would become part of the Great Sioux War (1876–1877), called for three military columns to advance into the remote vastness of the Northern Great Plains—parts of modern-day North and South Dakota, Montana, and Wyoming—where these scattered bands lived. The army's senior leaders were all experienced Civil War veterans, but a decade on the plains had made them little wiser in combat with Indians. Their methods of combat were far removed from the European styles for which these West Point graduates had been trained. The exception may have been Brigadier General George Crook, the head of the Department of the Platte and probably the army's most experienced Indian fighter. He defeated the Paiutes during a two-year conflict in the Pacific Northwest and, beginning in 1871, waged a successful campaign against the Apache in Arizona Territory. Custer, of course, had his own experience on the Great Plains. The army also increasingly relied on less experienced and poorly trained soldiers. More often, the enlisted men were immigrants who were ill-suited for long campaigns and Indian fighting.[2]

Nonetheless, the three columns that Sheridan called for initiated their campaigns toward the Lakota and Northern Cheyenne camps. The Montana Column, commanded by Colonel John Gibbon, marched from Forts Ellis and Shaw in western Montana Territory. The Wyoming Column under Crook traveled north from Fort Fetterman. The Dakota Column, under Brigadier General Alfred H. Terry and including the 650 men of Custer's Seventh Cavalry, departed from Fort Abraham Lincoln to the east.

Departing on 1 March, Crook's men marched up the old Bozeman Trail for the Powder River country, but severe winter weather hindered his troops. Early in the operation, on 17 March, Colonel Joseph J. Reynolds, a highly experienced officer on both the plains and in the Civil War, led an attack on a camp of Northern Cheyennes on the Powder River that initially went in the army's favor, but the warriors soon recovered their village. Crook retreated to Fort Fetterman to regroup.[3] Meanwhile, in Dakota Territory, winter delayed the column's departure from Fort Abraham Lincoln. Worse for Custer, political storms in the east nearly denied him any role in the campaign.[4]

Returning from New York City on 15 February 1876, Custer paused in Saint Paul to meet with General Terry to discuss the upcoming operation, during which Custer would hold field command of the column. They planned to initiate the march on 6 April. Terry created a simple blueprint for their movement: locate a site up the Yellowstone River for a secure supply depot to serve as Custer's base. With an infantry contingent protecting the base, the Seventh Cavalry would maneuver against the Lakotas and Northern Cheyennes, a plan reminiscent of the Washita campaign in 1868.

Bad weather played havoc with George and Libbie Custers' travel schedule, however. Snow and ice closed the Northern Pacific line preventing the acquisition of supplies, but in March the railroad set up a special train to carry the Custers west to Bismarck. Extra engines, workers, and two snowplows pushed the train through the drifts. About sixty-five miles east of Bismarck, the whole enterprise bogged down. Just when it appeared all of them would have to wait for the spring thaw, a small battery and pocket telegraph relay were found in the Custers' car. Journalist Mark H. Kellogg, who was also a telegrapher, was onboard as well. The telegraph line was connected to the portable instrument, allowing the marooned train to make contact with Fargo and Fort Abraham Lincoln. Soon after, George's brother, Captain Thomas W. ("Tom") Custer, arrived by sleigh to retrieve his brother and sister-in-law and take them on to Bismarck, reaching the town on 13 March. The remaining passengers, including newspaper editor Clement A. Lounsberry and Kellogg, had to wait another week until the tracks were cleared.[5]

Custer's stay at the fort proved short. On 15 March, a telegram arrived ordering him to Washington to testify before the Congressional Committee on Expenditures in the War Department, also known as the Clymer Committee, named after its chair, Representative Heister Clymer of Pennsylvania. Although Secretary of War William W. Belknap had resigned to escape impeachment, the Clymer Committee kept investigating. Custer's testimony on 29 March and 4 April 1876 about his knowledge of post traderships amounted to little more than hearsay. He hoped to return quickly to Fort Abraham Lincoln to oversee preparations for the coming operation, but the possibility he might still be called to testify at Belknap's impeachment forced him to remain in Washington until 20 April.[6]

Shortly after departing the capital on 4 May, Custer received a politically motivated summons to return and await further orders from General William T. Sherman. Custer had stirred up the wrath of President Grant, whose brother was also implicated in the scandals. Grant angrily ordered Custer's removal from command of the entire expeditionary force as Terry had first planned and, eventually, the Seventh Cavalry, the ultimate insult for Custer. Terry would replace him as the expedition's overall commander. Major Marcus A. Reno, already in charge of the Seventh in Custer's absence, would lead the regiment. Even Custer's high-ranking friends, Sherman and Sheridan, could not extricate him from this dilemma. "By publicly attacking the president's official and personal family," historian Robert M. Utley observes, "Custer had lent himself to partisan Democratic purposes and now everyone fell in line to carry out the president's determination to punish him."[7]

Sherman, Sheridan, and Terry were aghast at the prospect of having Reno lead the Seventh. Terry, while a highly competent Civil War veteran, had never campaigned against Indian bands. Knowing Custer was his most experienced Indian fighter, Terry dictated a telegram to the president appealing for reinstatement of the contrite Custer. Fortunately for Custer and his superiors, opposition newspapers were pummeling Grant, who had little political choice but to restore Custer to his regimental command on 8 May. Custer could not have been more enthusiastic about the news.

About 5:00 AM on 17 May, the Dakota expedition, with Terry as the overall commander, marched through the Fort Abraham Lincoln parade ground on the plains near the Missouri River and headed up the bluffs. On the regiment's ride to their camp on the Heart River that first day, Libbie accompanied George, who was decked out in his fringed buckskin trousers and shirt with a red necktie as he wore so many times before. Under a light-flat-topped sombrero, his golden-red hair was cut short. Libbie returned to the fort the next day with the sutler's party. Leading his regiment into the field, Custer was in his element once again.[8] Terry, meanwhile, expressed his own confidence for the campaign's success to Sheridan. "I have no doubt of the ability of my column to whip all the Sioux whom we can find," he wrote.[9]

When historians sit down to pen their story of Custer's final battle in June 1876, they follow a familiar outline. Custer, an ambitious former general, led his regiment of some 650 decently armed and trained Seventh Cavalry troopers against a peaceful village of Lakota, Northern Cheyenne, and other Indian bands, consisting of fifteen hundred or more warriors and as many as ten thousand dependents, encamped along the Little Big Horn River in southeastern Montana. They had gathered under the leadership of the charismatic Hunkpapa spiritual leader Sitting Bull. The three army columns first had to find them and keep them from splitting into smaller bands to disappear into the western vastness.

Leading off was Colonel Gibbon, commander of the District of Montana and a superb officer during the Civil War. Departing Fort Ellis on 1 April, he and nearly five hundred soldiers headed east following the Yellowstone River. By mid-May, Gibbon's Crow scouts and their leader, Lieutenant James H. Bradley, had located the village in the Tongue River Valley in southeastern Montana. Eleven days later, the scouts repeated their success, pinpointing the camp in the Rosebud Valley, eighteen miles away. Yet, Gibbon failed to act twice. His troops could not cross the Yellowstone and, in dispatches to Terry, he made no mention of his scouts' discovery of the almost four hundred lodges with about three thousand people, including at least eight hundred fighters.

Unknown to army leaders, the village kept growing. Lakotas were leaving the various agencies in Dakota Territory and heading for the Powder River country. By the time Custer located the village in June, it stretched out for almost four miles along the Little Big Horn River, likely one of the largest villages ever seen in the region. Custer caught many of the villagers idling mid-afternoon on 25 June. If not napping, a number of its inhabitants, particularly women, children, and the elderly, were preoccupied with camp or family chores. The warriors in the village at the time were resting. Those fighters not present were away hunting in the surrounding wilderness.

The village itself could not be considered a single entity. Historian Michael Donahue notes that, at that time, members of every tribe commonly called "the Sioux" had gathered there.[10] The Lakotas, who lived primarily in Dakota, Montana, and Wyoming territories, made up the largest numbers. Many lived at the agencies on the Great Sioux Reservation, while segments of Lakota subtribes clung to their traditional ways in nomadic hunting bands under such leaders as Sitting Bull and Crazy Horse.

Other tribal groups joined these Lakotas, predominantly Oglalas, after they learned of the federal government's ultimatum to take up residence on the reservations. The Northern Cheyennes, in the wake of the Battle of Powder River that March, joined the Oglalas. Next came the Hunkpapas, Miniconjous, and Sans Arcs. In time, Blackfeet Lakotas, some Assiniboines, and Brulés as well as Southern Cheyennes inflated the size of the growing camp. By early June 1876, the village had six growing tribal circles.

About one week before Custer located this village, a combined Indian force fought General Crook's Wyoming column to a draw at the Battle of the Rosebud on 17 June. After this fight, more and more agency members continued to join Sitting Bull's group. Donahue described the camp's atmosphere as "much like a family reunion."[11] By 25 June 1876, the camp had made its way down Rosebud Creek and spread out along the Little Big Horn River, a long-time favorite summer encampment site for these bands. The number of warriors Custer faced has always been an elusive figure to pin down, but Donahue estimates it to have been between fifteen hundred and two thousand.[12]

The Lakotas, Cheyennes, and their allies thought the village's size afforded them protection. None of its inhabitants truly believed that any white soldiers would attack them at that time. While the Grant administration's statements of the previous fall should have served as a warning for the Indians peacefully encamped along the Little Big Horn, it was only one indicator of the changes coming their way. Perhaps some of their leaders sensed the transformations around them, especially the vanishing bison herds that always supplied the resources that supported them. In the year 1500, an estimated thirty million bison roamed the North American plains. By 1890, just fourteen years after the Little Big Horn, a mere five hundred may have remained.[13]

After leaving Fort Abraham Lincoln, the Dakota Column followed earlier trails from 1873 and 1874, but found no signs of the Indian camps. Custer was nevertheless in high spirits, often blazing trails for the column or participating in hijinks with his younger brothers, Tom and Boston. A spring blizzard on 1 June delayed the troops for a couple of days, but two days later, Gibbon's scouts located Terry's column. The latter unit pushed ahead to meet Gibbon's force at the Powder River on 9 June.

With Gibbon's information about the encampment's location, Terry began altering his plans. Much to Custer's chagrin, the general opted to send Major Reno on a scout up the Powder River and back down the Tongue River to rule out the presence of the Lakotas and Cheyennes in that area. Reporter Mark Kellogg suggested Custer was in a snit about his superior's plans. "General Custer declined to take command of the scout of which Major Reno is now at the head of," he reported, "not believing that any Indians would be met with in either direction. His opinion is that they are in bulk in the vicinity of the Rosebud range."[14]

For six days during Reno's absence, the command moved toward its rendezvous with Gibbon. It stopped briefly at the mouth of the Powder River to reorganize, including boxing up their sabers and storing them on board the riverboat *Far West*. Terry expected Reno's return by 15 June at the Tongue River, but the major did not show. Instead, on 19 June, Reno sent Terry a message detailing his scout. After checking the Tongue and Powder valleys, Reno moved over to the Rosebud. He then headed north to the Yellowstone, where he waited for his commander.

Despite his enterprise, Reno found himself roundly criticized for exceeding his orders instead of being praised for providing Terry with his best information about the village's whereabouts. Both Kellogg and Custer wrote disparaging letters that posthumously appeared in the *New York Herald*. In a column from 11 July, Kellogg insisted, "For some cause unknown to your correspondent, Major Reno was unfortunate enough not only to exceed but to disobey the orders and instructions of General Terry."[15]

Kellogg's remarks mirrored Custer's own. Appearing the same day, Custer's anonymously written editorial lambasted the major. "Reno, after an absence of 10 days, returned," Custer penned, "when it was found to the disgust of every member of the entire expedition, from the commanding general down to the lowest private, that Reno, instead of simply failing to accomplish any good results, had so misconducted his force as to embarrass, if not seriously and permanently mar, all hopes of future success of the expedition."[16] In reality, recent camp sites that Reno found suggested the village, previously spotted by Lieutenant Bradley, had moved up Rosebud Creek sometime earlier. That movement meant Terry had to revise his plan for catching the camps there.

Two days later, on 21 June, Terry gathered Custer, Gibbon, and the latter's subordinate, Major James Brisbin, in a cabin on the *Far West* as it was moored on the Yellowstone River at the mouth of the Rosebud. Under the general's new plan, Custer's regiment would function as a strike force by traveling up Rosebud Creek following the Indian trail. In the meantime, the rest of Terry's force and Gibbon's column would march up the Yellowstone to the Bighorn River. Next, moving south along the Bighorn, they would take up blocking positions at the Little Big Horn. Once Custer's men located the village, the Seventh Cavalry would attempt to drive the Lakotas, Cheyennes, and their allies north toward the combined components of Terry and Gibbon, trapping them. The plan's success depended on Custer detecting the encampment. Terry could not discount the possibility that the tribes might have already turned east up the Rosebud and headed back toward Dakota Territory.

Terry's written orders have often engendered controversy. Many historians condemn Custer for failing to follow his general's instructions. In truth, Terry's circumstances were so fluid that Custer required the freedom to make decisions in the saddle. "It is of course impossible to give you any definite instructions in regard to this movement," he told Custer, "and were it not impossible to do so, the Department Commander places too much confidence in your zeal, energy, and ability to wish to impose upon you precise orders, which might hamper your action when nearly in contact with the enemy."[17] Whatever Terry meant to say, Custer clearly believed he was free to make decisions as his circumstances dictated. At the moment that he presented those instructions, Terry undoubtedly intended to afford Custer significant flexibility. Only after Custer died did the negative political and military feedback give Terry pause about what he meant. The controversy about whether Custer exceeded his orders remains a point of debate even today.

As Terry and his subordinates prepared along the Yellowstone, they remained unaware of Crook's recent setback that would impact them all. Early on the morning of 17 June, while Crook and the 1,350 men in his Wyoming Column camped for coffee farther south along Rosebud Creek, as many as a thousand warriors led by Crazy Horse launched a surprise attack on the soldiers. The fighting raged across the wide battlefield for much of the day, but resulted in light casualties on both sides. Their fighting done, the warriors withdrew. Crook remained in control of the field and claimed a rather hollow victory. Instead of continuing his northward march toward Terry's and Gibbon's units, however, Crook reversed course. Turning south, he encamped along Goose Creek in the area of modern-day Sheridan, Wyoming, to care for his wounded and await resupply. At a critical moment for the campaign, he removed his troops from the theater and remained idle for several weeks. Of greater concern, although his options were few, he failed to alert his fellow commanders that the warriors were more numerous and definitely more aggressive than the army expected.

The Terry column made its next move five days later on 22 June. Terry may have expected that Custer could be in position by 26 June, providing sufficient time for Gibbon's troops to reach their post along the Little Big Horn. The Seventh Cavalry departed from the Yellowstone River, going up Rosebud Creek in pursuit of the Indians. Terry and Gibbon headed west along the Yellowstone, then turned south along the Bighorn River toward the mouth of the Little Big Horn a few days later. Terry hoped to be in position on 26 June to entrap any refugees Custer forced north. All of the campaign's leaders still lacked a critical piece of intelligence about their enemy—the Indians' strength had grown steadily through-out the month.

For his advance up the Rosebud, Custer's regiment con-sisted of 597 soldiers, plus 50 scouts and civilians. Only the mule-borne pack train prevented an even quicker move in the rugged Rosebud backcountry.[18] Custer kept his Crow and Ree scouts active for the next three days seeking signs of the enemy. By 24 June, they reported that the village was likely on the lower reaches of the Little Big Horn. Before dawn on 25 June, they scaled a high point in the Wolf Moun-tains known as the Crow's Nest and spotted unmistakable signs of a large pony herd roaming in the Little Big Horn Valley, some fifteen miles to the west.[19]

Following a night march, Custer rode ahead of his col-umn, joining his scouts at the Crow's Nest. The feature stands as one of the truly significant sites associated with Custer's last day. The historical record substantiates that on the morning of 25 June, Custer climbed this high precipice. From this ridge top, he gazed west, seeking his first glimpse of his enemy's encampment. Custer could not make out either the Indians' massive pony herd or the smoke of the camps as his scouts could, but he believed their report that the camp lay ten miles or more to the west. Relying on his scouts' word, he organized his regiment for its final move-ment to engage the Lakotas and their allies. The Crow's Nest effectively served as the opening act in the Battle of the Little Big Horn.

Custer first planned an early morning attack for the fol-lowing day. Eight years earlier at the Battle of the Washita, he successfully struck Black Kettle's village at dawn from multiple directions. Now, in 1876, he wanted to repeat that successful strategy. New information soon altered his think-ing about when to attack and likely influenced the battle's outcome that afternoon, however. Custer feared Indian hunting parties had spotted his regiment and that his elusive foe would flee before the army could corral them. He therefore opted for a more dangerous midday attack on 25 June.[20]

His command crossed the divide between Rosebud Creek and the Little Big Horn River and began its march down the valley of what is known today as Reno Creek. Soon, Custer halted his troops.[21] He ordered Captain Frederick W. Benteen and the 115 men of Companies D, H, and K to ride southwest, over a series of rugged ridges and coulees to attack any Indians or outlying villages he might discover. In handing this assignment to Benteen, Custer was clearly influenced by circumstances from the Washita. During that fight, Cheyenne warriors from outlying villages downstream unexpectedly attacked Custer. In 1876, he was being more cautious. According to Custer's orders, Benteen was to countermarch to rejoin the regiment's main body if he did not find the enemy.

In further dividing the unit, Custer assigned companies A, G, and M to Reno and companies C, I, and L to Captain Myles W. Keogh. Companies E and F were under Captain George W. M. Yates. An augmented Company B, under Captain Thomas M. McDougall, would protect the slow-moving, mule-borne pack train.

Many Custer critics believe he erred by dividing his regiment. Yet, such tactics were common among the army's senior leadership in that period. If anything, Custer went "by the army book." He also has been criticized for not conducting a more thorough scout to ascertain his enemy's strength. Although a valid judgement in one sense, it fails to recognize that he feared the Lakotas and Cheyennes had spotted his troops and would scatter before he engaged them. In crossing the divide, he had not yet committed to the attack, but his take-charge attitude would not hold him back depending on the circumstances.

In viewing Custer's decision, historians seldom consider another critical factor. At the Battle of Powder River three months earlier, Colonel Reynolds had failed to complete his conquest of a village of Northern Cheyennes, who retook their village when Reynolds retreated. In response, Crook charged Reynolds with a series of offenses. In January 1877, a court-martial convicted Reynolds on three of them—disobedience of orders, abandoning his dead on the field of battle, and failure to recapture the Indian pony herd. The guilty verdict effectively ended his career and Reynolds retired from the army on 25 June 1877.[22]

Custer was a far superior and more aggressive commander compared to Reynolds. Undoubtedly, he was aware of Reynolds's problems at Powder River. Even so, Custer had a different mindset about battling any foe. When he responded to combat situations, he largely made the correct decision. Only reluctantly in the Civil War had he ever retreated. At perhaps his most tenuous moment of command in the rebellion, the Battle of Trevilian Station, Virginia, Custer kept his wits about him and continued an aggressive search for his enemy's weakness and his own escape. Even if Custer had accepted his scouts' advice about the size of the enemy force that lay before them in 1876, under no circumstance would he have pulled back and later sought to explain his action to his superiors. Additionally, if he held back and waited for Terry and Gibbon, more than likely the large village would have begun breaking up as the Little Big Horn landscape could not sustain that number of humans and animals for long. Likely, Custer never considered holding back at that moment on 25 June because he thought the Indians were too strong to engage. Doing so was not part of his make-up.

All the army's senior leaders in 1876 assumed that the Indians would flee rather than face a massive attacking force when confronted. After the Battle of the Rosebud, Crook never advised Terry and Custer that this native force had changed its tactics. They were more likely to stand and fight. Although Custer's scouts had alerted him to the camp's growing numbers, he failed to heed their warnings. He was confident that his regiment was up to its assigned task. Of significance as well, battlefield archaeological projects conducted in the 1980s confirmed that the Lakotas and their allies were well-armed, much more so than army commanders expected.

Attacking at midday, Custer came upon a village that, at least figuratively, was napping and unable to flee. Instead, the warriors stood and fought to defend their people. Often writers claim that Custer lost because he faced a superior foe. That assertion may have been true, in part, as the Indians forced Custer to engage them on poor ground for cavalry action. They also heavily outnumbered the 210 men directly under Custer, although they never deployed their superior strength against the other elements of the Seventh Cavalry. Many reasons are put forth for why the warriors did not later try to overwhelm the remaining forces of Reno and Benteen, including the need to maintain their fighting core. In any case, the Indians had the numbers, they had the firepower, and they had the desire to fight that day at the Little Big Horn.

Two hours after joining his scouts at the Crow's Nest, Custer was several miles closer to the Little Big Horn and facing his next crucial decision. Interpreter-scout Fred Girard yelled to him from a small knoll near an abandoned Indian camp on the lower reaches of Reno Creek, "Here are your Indians, running like Devils." Ahead of the troops, Indian horsemen rode hard for the river. Custer ordered Reno and his 130 cavalrymen and 24 scouts to charge the group, erroneously assuming they were scattering warriors, women, and children.[23] Reno likely expected—perhaps mistakenly—that Custer would support him from the rear. Instead, Custer with Keogh's and Yates' battalions—numbering 220 men prior to the dispatch of two couriers, the departure of four Indian scouts, and the straggling of at least four troopers whose horses gave out—turned to the north and mounted the high bluffs east of the river. Lagging far behind Custer and Reno on the regiment's back trail were the 135 men of Captain McDougall's Company B, escorting the pack train. McDougall caught up only after the troops had engaged the Indians.

Custer's purpose for turning north remains unclear. Sergeant Daniel Kanipe, who carried a message from Custer urging on the pack train, thought Custer reacted to the appearance of some fifty to one hundred warriors on the high ground to his front.[24] Custer may have feared an Indian party was riding out to confront his soldiers, or he intended to follow the warriors into the village proper. According to Cheyenne accounts, a sizable band was moving east of the Little Big Horn, among them the warriors under Wolf Tooth and Big Foot. Likely other parties, of varying strength, were east of the river.[25]

Author Michael Donahue offers another possible reason for Custer's reaction. The Lakotas and Cheyennes on Custer's right flank may have been decoys to lure him into an ambush. This group also could have cut off his force from the pack train, similar to what had occurred at the Washita. Donahue concludes that Custer had "little choice but to ride forward in that direction in order to gather more information."[26] Donahue also notes that Custer did not communicate his change of plans to chase after the small group of warriors with his subordinates, similar to Major Joel H. Elliott's fatal movement in 1868.[27]

Elliott's death supposedly remained on the minds of the regiment's senior personnel, especially influencing the acerbic Captain Frederick W. Benteen. He had never liked his regimental commander, but had befriended Elliott while at Fort Harker the winter before Washita. Within weeks of that fight, Custer and Benteen clashed publicly after Benteen's letter to a friend, William DeGress, was published in both the *Missouri Democrat* and the *New York Times*. Benteen lambasted Custer for what he considered Custer's callous abandonment of Elliott.[28] Yet by 1876, only a few Washita veterans remained among the contingents under Reno and Benteen. Perhaps they wondered if they were enduring a repeat performance by their regimental commander. That idea all seems natural enough under the combat situation those June nights in 1876, but likely had no impact on the fighting. Still, the regiments' veterans of the Washita campaign may well have recalled the Elliott incident as they wondered about Custer's own absence on the night of 25 June.

Whether the controversy truly hindered Custer's regiment prior to the Little Big Horn seems highly doubtful. Historian Brian C. Pohanka put little credence into the episode's effects on the Seventh Cavalry's field performance, both before and during the battle.[29] Petty arguments and factionalism beset other regiments, notably the Fourth United States Cavalry under Colonel Ranald Mackenzie, as well. Particularly, these occurred among their ever-ambitious officers during a lengthy period when military promotions moved at a glacial pace. Even if conflict existed after Elliott's demise at the Washita among the officers in the Seventh Cavalry, it most likely would have had little effect on their performances.

Other theories abound about Custer's intentions at the Little Big Horn, but none of them involve the Elliott episode. Some battle students believe Custer planned to hit the village at its northern end in a classic pincer movement, catching the village between two parts of the regiment. A more recent theory holds that Custer sought to cut off the apparent flight of the women and children and seize them as hostages as he had done at the Washita. Custer's crucial decision to head north remains a key point of controversy. Whatever truly motivated Custer, his decision left Reno threatened and stranded in the valley, unaware of Custer's next move.

In acting, Custer undoubtedly still believed he controlled the combat situation. At that moment and with that decision, however, events would prove him wrong. When Reno's soldiers first appeared on the edge of their camps, the Indians may have been surprised, even stunned. In response to Reno, hundreds of warriors quickly rushed to defend their families and seized the momentum back from the cavalry, which stalled Reno's advance. The major, perhaps out of panic, grew hesitant as more warriors surged forward. His worry about how many fighters lay hidden in the huge village beyond added to his alarm.

In Reno's mind, he followed his orders to charge the enemy. Now, that foe appeared poised to overwhelm him with no support in sight. Reno dismounted his three companies and formed a skirmish line. As army protocol dictated, every fourth man grabbed the reins of his comrades' horses and led them into a nearby timbered area along the river to Reno's right, reducing his combat strength.

As warriors threatened the corners of his skirmish line, Reno feared the Indian force would overrun his position. After ten to fifteen minutes, pressure from the Lakotas and their allies forced Reno to skedaddle to new locations within the timber, actually more of a brushy area. Reno had dispatched two couriers to Custer warning him of his predicament. Some troopers claimed to have seen Custer's own men moving north on the bluffs across the river, but that did not reassure the major.

Within thirty minutes of the soldiers' entry into the timber, the Lakotas and Cheyennes were seriously pressing the major's fragile lines. Reno ordered his men to mount—his critics claim he panicked—and they dashed from the timber. The fighting retreat quickly degenerated into a chaotic stampede. Desperate troopers galloped for the hoped-for safety on top of the two hundred-foot bluffs beyond the river with Indians following in close pursuit. By the time Reno's exhausted survivors scaled the heights, nearly 40 percent of his men lay dead, wounded, or had been abandoned. In addition, some twenty Indian scouts had departed, placing Reno's overall loss at more than 50 percent.[30] With such casualties, his battalion ceased to be an effective fighting force.

Elsewhere, Benteen ended his maneuvers and followed the regiment's back trail. En route, he received two messages from Custer urging him to advance rapidly. Just as Reno's broken command reached the safety of the bluffs, Benteen's companies rode up. Some thirty minutes later, McDougall's pack train began to arrive. While Reno and Benteen reorganized their commands and established a defensive perimeter, pressure from the Lakotas and Cheyennes slowed. At the same time, heavy firing could be heard to the north. Clearly, Custer was engaged.

One of the messages Benteen received instructed him to come quickly and bring the packs, especially those with extra ammunition. Today, he is still criticized for his failure to reinforce Custer's detachment. Neither Reno nor Benteen showed any inclination to ride toward the sound of the guns. Although many of their comrades claimed to have heard volley firing from the north, the two senior officers kept changing their stories. Three years later, by the time a court of inquiry was held at Reno's request, both men claimed to have heard only scattered firing at most.[31]

Angered by this seeming inaction, Captain Thomas B. Weir and his Company D headed for the fighting. His unauthorized move prompted other elements to begin a poorly coordinated advance. They joined Weir's troopers atop a high-top mini-ridge known today as Weir Point, about one mile north of Reno's original position and three miles from Custer's final one. Weir's men likely witnessed the last stages of Custer's battle. From that distance, however, the soldiers could not say what they saw.[32]

Soon, large groups of Indians rapidly rode toward the companies under Reno and Benteen. Their impromptu force quickly fell back to their original position. Only one man, Vincent Charley of Company D, was killed in this chaotic withdrawal. An effective rearguard action by Lieutenant Edward S. Godfrey and his dismounted Company K enabled the command to escape. As the troopers dug in for a protracted siege, some wondered about the whereabouts of Custer's command. Most believed he, too, had been besieged or had continued north to join the combined forces under Terry and Gibbon.

For the rest of that day and most of the next, Reno's and Benteen's seven companies endured a deadly sniping fire, adding to their casualties.[33] Acting Assistant Surgeon Henry R. Porter cared for the battalion's wounded in a make-shift hospital that he had set up in a swale at the center of the defensive site and that was partially sheltered from the enemy fire by mules and horses. The cavalrymen obtained water by dangerously descending the bluffs to the Little Big Horn, then climbing back to that position. Occasionally, the Lakotas and Cheyennes directly engaged the soldiers in their lightly fortified positions. Benteen, who receives more credit than Reno for overseeing the line's successful defense, personally led a charge that repulsed one such foray.

Before Reno's retreat from the valley, Custer rode to the top of a rise known today as Sharpshooter Ridge. As he and several men looked down on the village below, the warriors appeared to be missing.[34] Reno's final messenger, Private John Mitchell, arrived to update Custer that the Indian force was challenging Reno. Unfortunately for the command, the bluffs blocked Custer's view of that action, even though Custer reportedly told his troops, "Hurrah, boys, we've got them! We'll finish them up and then go home to our station."[35] Custer could not have been further from the truth.

As the cavalry moved forward at a fast clip, at least two privates, Peter Thompson and James Watson, were forced to drop out. Captain Tom Custer gave Kanipe an order for the pack train and Benteen's battalion to hustle them along. Custer needed every man in the upcoming fight. In the meantime, the five companies descended what became known as Cedar Coulee and entered Medicine Tail Coulee. Turning left, they next headed for the river.

Custer's concerns were mounting. If cut off by the warriors, the pack train remained vulnerable on the back trail. Realizing his own supply of ammunition was too sparse, Custer stopped the column and had the regimental adjutant, Lieutenant W. W. Cooke, hastily scrawl a six-line note that a young Italian-born trumpeter named Giovanni Martini—known as John Martin—carried to Benteen. The note read: "Benteen Come On. Big Village. Be quick. Bring pacs. W.W. Cooke P.S. Bring packs."[36] When Martin, the last man to see Custer alive, departed the battalion about 3:20 PM, the head of the cavalry column was about to enter the Medicine Tail Coulee Valley. Like Kanipe, who had left ten to fifteen minutes earlier, Martin recalled that Custer's troopers were enthusiastic. Riding their horses at a rapid gait, the men were cheering. Custer himself appeared jubilant when he saw the village's lodges standing and still vulnerable to attack.[37]

Martin later linked up with the regiment's rear elements and survived the fighting. Similarly, Donahue outlines, several other men effectively received last-minute reprieves that day through equally quirky circumstances. Two privates, Edwin Pickard and Charles Banks, for example, were ordered to take extra horses back to the pack train and consequently survived.

Less fortunate was Custer's own brother, Boston, who had been on detail with the pack train. Martin passed Boston near Weir Point as he rode to the front at a hard clip. Martin also hailed Benteen's men watering their horses at a place now called the Morass along Reno Creek. Boston caught up to the five companies and his body was found on the slope on Last Stand Hill near those of his older brothers. The youngest Custer surely would have informed his brother of Benteen's whereabouts.

As Martin headed for the rear, he took one last glance at his comrades back in Medicine Tail Coulee. They appeared to be falling back from the river. As his courier departed, Custer followed the coulee toward the river and a ford opposite the Cheyennes' encampment at the northern edge of the village, some 1.6 miles to the west. Cheyenne accounts describe an abortive attempt led by Company E (the Gray Horse Troop) to ford the Little Big Horn there. Other Lakotas and Cheyennes stated that Custer's soldiers never gained the river proper. Military officials who later inspected the field were equally divided in their impressions of this action. Some historians believe the detachment's movement was a feint designed to hold the warriors in place while the rest of Custer's force continued north to flank the village. Other writers, including Richard A. Fox, suppose that, with the encampment nearly empty as Custer approached the ford, moving north to intercept fleeing villagers made more sense than attacking a largely abandoned village.[38]

More recently, Donahue thinks that Custer's force reached the near bank of the Little Big Horn River, but could not cross because of quicksand. Heavy firing from warriors across the waterway forced them to fall back after an officer was either badly wounded or killed. Over the years, many accounts have claimed that Custer was the fallen officer. Pohanka firmly believed, however, that the Seventh Cavalry's actions from the river crossing until its end on Last Stand Hill meant that Custer remained in command.[39]

Custer earlier divided his battalion into two smaller wings, or squadrons, placing them under Keogh and Yates. One squadron, generally assumed to have been Yates's command, may have approached the ford. Meanwhile, Keogh with the other three companies moved northward along Blummer/Nye-Cartwright Ridge. During this movement, some fighting occurred along the rise, possibly with the Wolftooth/Big Foot band. In the 1940s, the superintendent of the recently established Custer (now Little Bighorn) Battlefield National Monument, Edward Luce, discovered a line of expended carbine shells on a ridge north of Medicine Tail Coulee. Luce's findings indicate an initial skirmish there with either outriding warriors or possibly the villagers fleeing east across the river as a result of Reno's attack. Since only a few slain soldiers were later found in the vicinity, they likely faced long-range firing. The decisive battle was waged more than half a mile to the north.[40]

After exchanging some distant fire with small bands of warriors, Keogh's three companies headed north to reunite on Calhoun Hill, a high point at the southeast end of a ridge now known as Battle Ridge, with Yates's two companies. That knoll would have been a logical place for Custer to have made his own stand as he possibly could have controlled the situation better along those grounds. His northward progress was in keeping with Custer's aggressive temperament. Yet, circumstances during the fighting put Custer on the defensive. Even then, Custer continued to look for an advantage over his enemy. Donahue correctly notes that "Custer had a real dilemma." While the Lakotas and Cheyennes significantly outnumbered him, the regiment's firepower could have sustained a defense for some time. Instead, as Donahue acknowledges, "The real problem was his limited ammunition supply, soldiers without horses, and perhaps several wounded men."[41]

Archaeological evidence supports Cheyenne oral traditions describing a movement, most likely of Yates's squadron, to the vicinity of another crossing point northwest of the present-day National Park Service battlefield museum and Custer National Cemetery. From that position, the soldiers threatened many women, children, and elderly villagers who had sought shelter in the trees and brush on the river's west bank. When the Lakota and Cheyenne forces began pressuring Keogh's three companies near Calhoun Hill, Custer was forced to wage an increasingly desperate defensive battle.[42]

Distressed by this turn in fortune, Custer returned to his bag of tricks used at the Washita, where he seized some fifty women and children as hostages. In the valley below, an old river meander that Donahue labels variously as Chasing Creek, Squaw Creek, or Squaw Ravine provided shelter to hundreds, if not thousands, of Indian noncombatants. From their position, the cavalrymen immediately threatened these people. Turning his focus to them, Custer dispatched a unit toward the river and Chasing Creek, hoping his troopers could capture some of those refugees.[43]

Donahue states that the episode may have involved as many as two companies, but a smaller detachment seems more likely, given Custer's manpower shortage in the moment. It was Custer's last desperate move and one doomed to fail. The Lakotas and Cheyennes from across the field, sensing Custer's plan, rushed to the ravine. Their heavy volley blunted the cavalry's advance and killed several men, including reporter Mark Kellogg.[44] The surviving soldiers either took refuge in another ravine, known as Deep Ravine, or fought back toward the high point now known as Last Stand Hill.

Firing from the vicinity of Calhoun Hill told of Indian successes elsewhere on the field as they stormed the remaining positions of the Seventh Cavalry. Some Indian accounts credit the Cheyenne war leader Lame White Man's decisive charge over Battle Ridge to the rear of Custer's final position with precipitating the ultimate collapse of the entire contingent. This attack may have occurred as Company C moved forward from Calhoun Hill toward the Little Big Horn in an attempt to scatter the growing Lakota and Cheyenne force massing behind the cover of Greasy Grass Ridge to the southeast. Out in the open, the troopers became more vulnerable to the series of counterattacks. Company C had deployed in line when the Indians struck and drove them back toward Calhoun Hill. The Brulé Lakota Two Eagles recalled that "some of the soldiers were mounted and some were dismounted. Most of those dismounted had lost their horses."[45]

This sudden reversal exposed Keogh's wing. The cavalrymen on Calhoun Hill came under heavy pressure from their front and flank. Lieutenant James Calhoun and Lieutenant John Crittenden urged their men on, but the warriors' firepower and numbers proved too strong. Behind them was

Horse Holder's Ravine, where the remaining mounts were protected and the regiment may have set up a make-shift hospital. Other Indian fighters, covered by the ridges to the east, unleashed a severe fire on Keogh's Company I before his men could fully react to the impending disaster. With every fourth trooper detailed as a horse-holder, the dismounted company's skirmish lines were dangerously thin and the horses presented a vulnerable target. The men who managed to survive these final routs desperately raced for Last Stand Hill. In his testimony before the army court of inquiry in 1879, Benteen asserted that the scattered disposition of the dead on the hillside revealed the clash to have been "a rout, a panic, till the last man was killed."[46] Private Jacob Adams shared this view, later stating, "We came to the conclusion then and there that the fight had been a rout, a running fight."[47]

Many Indian accounts reinforce this impression of chaos and annihilation. "Horses were running over the soldiers and over each other," the Cheyenne fighter Wolftooth remembered. "The fighting was really close and they were shooting almost without taking aim."[48] Low Dog, an Oglala warrior, likewise recalled the soldiers "did very poor shooting." In an apparent reference to the horse holders, he noted, "Their horses were so frightened that they pulled the men all around, and a great many of their shots went up in the air and did us no harm."[49]

On Last Stand Hill, Custer found himself with only one option. He ordered surviving horses shot to form a barricade and afford his remaining men some protection. The Seventh Cavalry's ammunition was almost gone, however, and the warriors vastly outnumbered them. At one point, Donahue surmises, the knot of men desperately looking for assistance may have seen Weir and others of Reno's command three miles away on Weir Point. Outnumbered and out of bullets, the men on Last Stand Hill, including Custer, fell to the onslaught of Lakota and Cheyenne firepower.

After inspecting the field in the days after the clash, Benteen claimed to have counted some seventy dead cavalry horses on the rise. He counted just two dead Indian ponies —not impossible given that the Lakotas and Cheyennes generally preferred stealthy infiltration on foot to head-on mounted assaults. These details suggest that the Indians wiped out the troopers before they assumed a cohesive defensive position. Many battle students believe that no more than fifty Indians died in the fighting, with some setting the figure at fewer than forty. The fact that the Indians successfully removed their dead from the field has fueled the continuing debate over how many warriors died.[50]

More than likely, the intense, close-quarters combat followed an extended period of tactical maneuver and seeming stability on the Seventh Cavalry's part. Many Indians first engaged Reno prior to turning north to meet the new threat that Custer posed. It clearly took time for warrior strength to build against his five companies. Once they had sufficient numbers, the Indians more or less simultaneously lashed out across the field. This tactic prevented Custer from concentrating his dispersed companies in a tight defensive perimeter that might have enabled his outnumbered force to hold off the onslaught, as he had done along the Yellowstone three years earlier.

The first significant concentration of dead cavalrymen, some fifteen troopers, was found at the southwestern corner of the battlefield. On the rise northeast of this position lay deceased soldiers of Company L, including Custer's brother-in-law, Lieutenant Calhoun. Witnesses reported that Calhoun's men appeared to deploy in a skirmish line. People who later scoured the field found twenty-five to forty expended carbine shells scattered around the bodies. Clearly, Calhoun's troopers had maintained a stable position and fought fiercely before being overrun.[51]

On the exposed eastern slope of Battle Ridge, halfway between Calhoun and Last Stand hills, Keogh's body was identified amid a pile of slain troopers. One of his trumpeters was sprawled across the captain's corpse. His two sergeants, guidon bearer, and orderly also laid nearby. Most of the dead men in this group seemed to have belonged to Keogh's Company I, mixed with a few men from companies C and L. The remains of soldiers from several companies—likely those comprising Keogh's wing or squadron—were scattered up the slope from their initial position toward Last Stand Hill.[52]

Atop the rise and strewn down its western face were the bodies of George and Tom Custer, Custer's adjutant W. W. Cooke, Yates, and the bulk of his Company F. The presence of First Lieutenant Algernon Smith of Company E, the Gray Horse Troop, a considerable distance from the dead of his company, indicates that he was an early casualty. Godfrey stated that forty-three dead were found on Last Stand Hill. Thirty-nine dead horses along the slopes indicated to observers that they had been killed to form an impromptu barricade, marking where Custer chose to make his last stand.[53]

The only other large concentration of dead was found several hundred yards southwest of Last Stand Hill in the upper recesses of Deep Ravine. Numerous witnesses counted twenty-eight bodies there, among whom were First Sergeant Frederick Hohmeyer and seven others belonging to Company E. Four of the eight identified dead were non-commissioned officers. Several troopers from Company F were also tentatively identified in the vicinity of Deep Ravine, though most of them were logically assumed to be Company E men. Whether as the result of a tactical deployment gone awry or a desperate attempt to escape, these cavalrymen had been cut off and forced to wage their own last stand in that narrow cul-de-sac.[54]

Near the foot of Last Stand Hill lay Custer's youngest brother Boston and his nephew Arthur Reed. Scattered bodies—Captain McDougall said no more than a dozen— were found between the hill and Deep Ravine. Some of those men may have been fugitives from the last stand, making their way toward soldiers holding out in the ravine, an event many Indian veterans recounted after the fight. On the flats near the river, Colonel Gibbon discovered Kellogg's body. The little mutilation inflicted on the slain correspondent suggests he was an early casualty. If he had been among the last survivors, he would have attracted more attention.[55]

Unfortunately for future historians, no detailed, accurate maps were drawn outlining the locations of the dead men and horses or of the carbine shells scattered about the field. Indeed, no one was ever quite sure how many corpses were interred on the battleground or how many were overlooked. Most witnesses seem to have shared the sentiments of Captain Walter Clifford of Gibbon's Seventh United States Infantry Regiment who wrote in his diary, "Let us bury our dead and flee from this rotting atmosphere."[56]

By the evening of 26 June, the Lakotas and Cheyennes had ceased their attacks on Reno's besieged units. Soon, the cavalrymen watched as the huge column of warriors and their families streamed southwest across the valley floor toward the distant Bighorn Mountains. By dawn on 27 June, the valley was empty. About 11:00 AM, the survivors spotted Terry's and Gibbon's columns advancing through the abandoned village. Any joy the men on the bluffs felt at their rescue was short-lived. The relief party also brought word that they had discovered the bodies of Custer and his dead comrades on the hills downstream.

6

After the Little Big Horn

Just slightly more than ten days after the battle, sometime before midnight on 5 July 1876, John Piatt Dunn, the first druggist and an early political leader in Bismarck, Dakota Territory, recalled that a voice out front of his rough house filtered through his open screen door. "Doc," it called several times, "The next words I heard were, 'Custer and his whole command has been massacred to a man!'" He recollected in an 1894 interview, "I was stunned, for a moment, absolutely. It seemed incredible."

Earlier that night, the steamer *Far West* had returned to the young pioneer settlement on the Missouri River with its sorrowful news about the Battle of the Little Big Horn. "It was a moonlight [*sic*] night, a fall harvest moon, and very warm," Dunn remembered. Venturing outside his home, he found the streets filled. "The excitement was intense," he said, "and the gloom and grief when the news was confirmed, and when the wounded and attendants were brought off the boat, cannot be understood now—one must have been here to realize the feeling which existed."[1]

George Custer's final battle had occurred on the ridges above the Little Big Horn River in southeastern Montana, several hundred miles west of Bismarck. In 1876, the town remained small and at the edge of the frontier, only three years removed from its founding when the Northern Pacific Railroad extended its tracks to the Missouri River. Its citizens knew one another well. They were also quite familiar with Custer and the men of his Seventh United States Cavalry stationed across the river at Fort Abraham Lincoln. Not surprisingly, as Dunn's comments indicate, Custer's defeat stunned people, both in Bismarck and across a nation in the midst of its centennial celebration. Author James E. Mueller has pointed out that Custer's loss in 1876 is likely "the enduring memory of the centennial year for America," whereas the usually dominant news event of any four-year cycle, the presidential campaign, today interests only political scientists and professional historians.[2]

The year 1876 was important for the United States, a young country still wrestling with its role on the world stage. The observance of its centennial amounted to a gala birthday celebration as the people sought to put the disaster of the Civil War behind them. The rebellion devastated the country's sense of purpose. Now, with the unpopular Reconstruction era nearing its close, the defeated southern states would soon have their full rights of participation in the country's life returned to them.

Many Americans held high expectations for future prosperity in the regions still officially classified as territories. This idea was especially true on the Northern Plains where Custer's formal discovery of gold in the Black Hills in 1874 had whetted the hopes of the nation's business interests for new riches. In Dakota Territory, expansionist-oriented boomers, such as the publisher and editor of the *Bismarck Tribune* Clement A. Lounsberry, strongly urged the federal government to open the hills to white settlement and development.

Undoubtedly, some government officials in early 1876 found themselves anchored in the midst of a moral dilemma—how to continue to recognize the treaty rights of American Indians amid the increasingly shrill calls of miners, ranchers, hunters, and railroads that urged expansion, no matter what the cost to the native populations.[3] Wresting the north country from the Lakotas, Northern Cheyennes, and other Plains Indians would be difficult and would require dispatching the army. In early 1876, no one in Bismarck, Washington, D.C., or any other city in the United

States could have imagined the catastrophe that would unfold in far-off Montana Territory. On a personal level that July evening in Bismarck, Dunn realized how disastrously the government's plans had worked out.

The story of the Battle of the Little Big Horn has become a mixture of myth and reality. Most important is the military story of the attack by Custer's Seventh Cavalry on the Indian village there and its violent outcome that resulted in the deaths of 268 United States soldiers and white civilians and from 40 to as many as 300 Lakotas and Cheyennes. Historians have focused on unraveling the whys and wherefores of the clash on 25 June 1876 and the larger conflict labeled as the Great Sioux War of 1876–1877, both of which have been well studied in the 145-year period since the Indian victory that day. Ever since the Seventh Cavalry's defeat, numerous stories and myths emerged surrounding Custer himself. With the Little Big Horn as the focus, numerous groups and individuals have argued over his death and his legacy.

Custer's legendary status in American history began with his Civil War exploits, even those prior to his actions in early July 1863 at Gettysburg and were refined on numerous fields of combat in the conflict's final twenty-one months. His many victories made it easy for him to sustain his heroic status. Of course, the war involved combat against southern white men in Pennsylvania, Maryland, and Virginia. Many of the men on both sides, as eyewitnesses to the violence, survived to write their own accounts of the units they had led or served with.[4] Anyone interested in the conflict does not lack for material about its history, its heroes, or its villains and countless volumes document Custer's deeds between 1861 and 1865. As historian Gregory J. W. Urwin states, "Custer certainly excelled in conventional set-piece engagements against Confederate troops. . . . The Civil War proved that he was not a rash fool and that his tactical bag of tricks contained a wider assortment than the head-long charge and the simple flank attack."[5]

Unfortunately for Custer's historical reputation and personal legend, he fought a second, much different war. As noted earlier, Custer achieved less success on the Great Plains in this next round of warfare. Historians, including Robert M. Utley and Louise Barnett, commonly blame Custer for his own mistakes during that period, especially when he was suspended from rank after a court-martial in 1867. A cottage industry of debate has grown up around his final engagement as well. Deliberations about the event itself threaten never to end, possibly stemming in part from changing views on the role of war in American culture since the last "good" war fought between 1941 and 1945.

Multiple other factors have altered Americans' scrutiny of how the nation has treated various groups over the centuries and what roles they should play going forward. "The Bands of Brothers" who fought from their foxholes of World War II never would have imagined that someday women would lead American troops in combat or that historic markers and statues dedicated to the Confederacy would be torn down by people who question the very notion of the existence of such icons. Today, many Americans, when meeting military veterans, reach out their hands in offering thanks for their service. One group of former fighters, however, remains lost on the western plains of the United States, condemned for their service to a country that still struggles with the reasons why those men were called to duty. At the head of the list of these soldiers is none other than George Custer. In his first war, he faced an enemy who enslaved other Americans of color and stood out as a hero. On the Great Plains, Custer found himself in a role reversal. He was now the one who waged war on an innocent minority and deserves history's condemnation.

Reporters in the years after Little Big Horn first contributed to the public's understanding of Custer's actions and death. Their reports can be divided into several phases. To begin, Clement Lounsberry dispatched his reporter Mark H.

Kellogg with Custer's column to report on the six-week campaign. Kellogg ended up dying on the flats close to the Little Big Horn and never got to write what some have referred to as "the Great Scoop."[6] Other reporters and many newspapers filled in the gap left by Kellogg's death. Robert Utley concluded that the American press "played an important part in the rise of the controversy." He argues, "Journalistic techniques in 1876 differed from those of today, and in the Little Big Horn 'massacre' the nation's press found a subject ideally suited to emotional treatment."[7] That view has been a staple for historians both before and since Utley's 1962 publication.

Most modern students of the battle accept the notion that the newspapers created the drama of the Little Big Horn more as it should have played out for Custer rather than how it actually happened. If the story were reported inaccurately and full of myths, the cause was simple. Kellogg was the only correspondent assigned to cover the Dakota Column. His singular status stemmed from Custer's own political problems with President Ulysses S. Grant prior to the campaign. After Grant rescinded Custer's removal from command of the Seventh Cavalry, General William T. Sherman dictated that no correspondents accompany Brigadier General Alfred H. Terry's force. Sherman advised Terry, "If you want General Custer along, [Grant] withdraws his objections. Advise Custer to be prudent," he continued, "not to take along any newspaper men, who always make mischief."[8]

As a result, many historians point at Custer and his apparently massive ego for having invited Kellogg to travel with the Dakota Column. That idea is not accurate. In July 1876, Lounsberry noted that Kellogg traveled as the expedition's only accredited correspondent at Terry's urging as he was "prepared to prove."[9] As the years passed, Lounsberry elaborated through his recollections. In August 1895, for example, Lounsberry wrote in his newspaper the *Fargo Record* that he "was the only correspondent invited by Custer to accompany the expedition."[10] In October 1911, he also told researcher Walter M. Camp that "Custer had furnished a horse and means of subsistence for Kellogg who went in my place, and he was known as the only correspondent."[11] When other newspapers, including the *New York Herald* and the *Chicago Tribune*, also claimed Kellogg as their correspondent after the battle, Lounsberry puffed indignantly that "the entire expense of outfitting Kellogg was borne, and all arrangements for his work were made by the *Bismarck Tribune*, and to it belongs the credit of sending with Terry the only newspaper correspondent."[12]

In more recent decades, the Associated Press itself has claimed Kellogg as its correspondent and its first one killed in action. That assertion is also inaccurate. No evidence exists to prove that Kellogg was an employee of the Associated Press in 1876. Lounsberry undoubtedly furnished stories from his newspaper to the organization and other eastern outlets for re-publication, as is still done today by associated news outlets. Neither Kellogg nor his surviving family members received any compensation from the wire service before or after his death.

By the summer of 1876, Captain William S. McCaskey, a Civil War veteran himself, already had some ten years of experience in the frontier army. In late April 1876, McCaskey and his company of the Twentieth United States Infantry had received orders to change stations from Fort Ripley, Minnesota, to Fort Abraham Lincoln. At the time, Terry and Custer prepared the Dakota Column for the summer campaign. McCaskey would command the fort in Custer's absence.[13]

In a letter dated 11 May 1876, McCaskey told his wife, Nellie, that Custer favorably impressed him. "I found Gen. Custer a much different man than I supposed him—without affectation or show and very considerate," he recorded. During the operation, Custer sent the captain an undated letter while en route to the Little Big Horn. Custer stated,

"Prospects of a fight on extensive scale each day diminishing." On the back, McCaskey noted it was the last letter he had received from Custer.

Not quite eight weeks after McCaskey wrote to his wife, the steamer *Far West*, carrying the wounded back from the Little Big Horn, docked late in the evening of 5 July in Bismarck for a couple of hours before embarking for the brief trip downriver to Fort Abraham Lincoln, arriving early the following morning. According to Second Lieutenant Charles L. Gurley's account of what followed, McCaskey first met with the fort's officers about 2:00 AM and asked for their assistance in telling the twenty-four families affected about the deaths of their loved ones. A little before seven o'clock that morning, post surgeon Johnson V. D. Middleton, McCaskey, and Gurley began their "sad errand" by waking up Libbie Custer's housemaid, Maria, and asking her to have Libbie, Custer's sister Margaret Calhoun, and his niece Emma Reed meet them in the parlor.

Gurley then described the reaction of the women after being informed of the deaths at the Little Big Horn. "Imagine the grief of those stricken women, their sobs, their flood of tears, the grief that knew no consolation," he wrote. After being told of her husband's fate, Libbie Custer sent for her wrap. Despite the heat of the day, the young widow shivered but she realized that, as the late commander's wife, she had a final duty to fulfill. Other women on the post were about to receive the same tragic message about their husbands and she would "stand by at the sad telling." Across the fort, Gurley recorded, all the residents moved anxiously about, fearful that a messenger would bring sad news their way. McCaskey later called it "the hardest duty I ever had to perform in the service."[14]

Even after taking on this difficult task, McCaskey continued to assist these widows as best he could. For example, he helped Libbie Custer, Maggie Calhoun, and the wife of Captain George W. M. Yates, Annie, file claims on life insurance policies their husbands had with the New York Life Insurance Company. Libbie received $4,750, apparently after a deduction of five percent for the risk of war. The Equitable Life Assurance Company sent a $3,000 check to George's parents, Emanuel and Maria Custer, as well.

On 30 July 1876, Libbie Custer left Fort Abraham Lincoln for the last time. In so doing, she removed herself from the protected cocoon of army life that had sheltered her for more than twelve years. She returned to her hometown of Monroe, Michigan, where her family, friends, and in-laws still lived. In the months that followed, others recorded, she was "prostrated with grief." As time eased her pain, many historians argue, she made it her personal mandate to assure that her husband was remembered in no less than glorious and heroic terms during the remaining fifty-seven years of her life. Libbie more than anyone else was responsible for transforming George Custer into a legendary icon.[15]

This image of Libbie as the all-domineering widow who time and again cowered George's friends and enemies from speaking an untoward public word about him, however, may have masked the depths of her despair and personal grief, especially in the early months after his death. In addition to her personal pain, Libbie now cared for her husband's elderly parents, who themselves lost three sons, a grandson, and a son-in-law that terrible Sunday afternoon. George's close friend, actor Lawrence P. Barrett, revealed how Libbie's grief and the responsibilities thrust onto her initially devastated the hardy widow.[16]

In Custer's life, no man outside of his family may have stood closer to him than Barrett. The two met in 1866 in Saint Louis, Missouri, and immediately struck up a friendship.[17] In 1874, Custer even invited Barrett to accompany his expedition to the Black Hills, but the actor gently turned down his friend's offer, citing his theater commitments.[18]

Barrett, once a Civil War captain, toured constantly during much of his acting career that only ended with his death in 1891.[19] During them, he wrote frequent, often lengthy letters to his wife, Mollie, who usually remained at their home in Massachusetts caring for their two daughters. In the fall of 1876, Barrett toured the Midwest, including Michigan. His series of letters home reveal both his deep need to see his friend's widow and his dread at fulfilling such a heart-wrenching obligation.

On 26 October, the actor laid out the emotional details of his sorrowful visit to pay his respects to Libbie the previous day. Barrett found her, "Oh! so changed! She was dressed in black—with great black lines to her sunken eyes and as pale as death—though not so much reduced in flesh as I expected." Mementos of the late general surrounded the two during the emotional two-hour encounter that was nearly too much for both the widow and the actor to handle. "We conversed upon his life, his death, and all things which concerned him," Barrett recorded. "She gave me the history of her affairs, as they stood, and I was so sorry to learn that the family will be left in struggling circumstances."

While Libbie hoped to support her aging in-laws, she clearly felt the dual pressures of her dire financial circumstances and her grief. Barrett described her as being "so broken that her whole strength is tasked to keep her mind free from insanity." Later in their discussion, she thought that, in time, she would write "some memorials" of her husband's life and might seek government employment. At that point, he took his leave of her and returned to his hotel, promising to return for a second visit later that day.

That afternoon, Emanuel called to guide Barrett to the family home. Barrett observed: "Before that hour the old gentleman came over, and upset me again—as he talked of 'his Boys'—his eyes filled with tears, his hands wandering—dazed—crushed and feeble—the mother [Maria] is still in bed dangerously ill." To Barrett, Emanuel seemed angry that the United States Congress refused to aid them, but had left all to Libbie, who was herself too feeble. "I assure you dear the scene of that old man's misery, poverty and loneliness after 'his Boys' will remain with me as long as I live, and the remembrance of the Massacre is made still more terrible by this."[20]

Barrett's second meeting with Libbie was no less emotional for them, but apparently she was more composed and revealing in her comments. First, she discussed the upcoming biography then being written by Frederick Whittaker. Historians speculate on Libbie's own role in steering Whittaker's writing, but are uncertain about the extent of her input.[21] Second, Barrett clearly positioned her in assuming her dominant role in protecting her husband's reputation, especially by emphasizing Major Marcus Reno's responsibility in Custer's death. "She will aid his Biographer in showing to the world that her dear Husband was 'sacrificed'— that Reno was a coward, by whose fault alone the dreadful disaster took place," Barrett wrote. She informed the actor that "her proofs are all in her possession now. When the proper moment arrives. she will demand an Investigation, and Gen'l Sheridan will grant it—then when she has cleared his fame—placed the blame of that 25th of June where it belongs, and settled his kindred comfortably—She will see to what further usefulness her life can be devoted."

Despite her statements of bravado, Libbie obviously passed through moments of more intense grief and depression. As Barrett articulated to his wife, "At one time she thought of suicide, but his [Custer's] presence was a reality —to warn her not to do such a deed, but to live for those they loved." Barrett added, "I could say but little."

Libbie also told Barrett of his own high ranking in Custer's life. "She told me how truly he loved me and that I was his closest and dearest friend," Barrett penned, "and then for his sake I asked that if we could ever aid her that she would let us do so." Soon, Maggie Calhoun, Emma Reed, and Emanuel Custer joined them. The moment was almost too much for the actor. "I leave you to imagine my feelings, dear, Sitting there with those three mourners, in black and with the childless Father.—I never thought I could pass through such an ordeal without breaking down. I came away at four—with blessings from them all as 'Autie's Friend.'"[22]

With few eyewitness accounts available of Custer's final moments, Captain Thomas B. Weir wished to provide Libbie Custer with his take on her husband's death. Several months after Little Big Horn, Weir wrote to her that if he could visit her, he would "tell you everything I know." Some Custer buffs think Weir intended to reveal all the secrets behind the disaster at the battle. Historian Shirley Leckie thinks that Weir more likely was referring to his own circumstances there. After Reno's retreat from the valley, Weir had not waited for the latter's permission before moving his company north to the sounds of the guns. Sadly, for history, Weir never visited Libbie Custer nor did he ever reveal what, if anything, he wished to tell her about his experience. Suffering from health problems related to alcoholism, Weir died on 9 December 1876, but never left his thoughts for historians to review.[23]

In her biography of George Custer, Louise Barnett points out that if he had returned to Fort Abraham Lincoln and learned of the death of his wife in his absence, his strong will and natural buoyancy likely would have supported him through his grief. He could have fallen back on his personal and military family, and he would have retained his rank and army standing.[24] On the other hand, George's death left a spouse who was truly unprepared for widowhood. When she was a child and later a single adult, her father closely watched over her. When Libbie married George, she gained a husband who cared deeply for her, even if his army status frequently left Libbie waiting anxiously for him to return. Now, in 1876, she no longer had a strong male figure in her life. At least initially in her widowhood, her husband's fumbling attempts at securing wealth through investments saddled her with more debts than cash in the bank. As a woman in the Victorian age, she was ill-prepared to earn a living for the rest of her life.

At first, such concerns may have weighed Libbie down and were responsible, in part, for the downtrodden figure who met with Barrett. Gradually, she took control of both her own life and the mythic afterlife of her late husband. Surprisingly, the impetus for her recovery and personal development as her husband's defender may have come from President Grant. Amid the post-battle controversies of the Little Big Horn, Grant stated, "I regard Custer's massacre as a sacrifice of troops, brought on by Custer himself, what was wholly unnecessary—wholly unnecessary."[25] Numerous other critics rose up to tarnish the Boy General's military standing as well. Such charges angered the young widow and gave her something to campaign against for her remaining years.

Historians often write that few critics dared to speak ill of George while Libbie still lived, but Lawrence A. Frost often disputed that notion. In his book *General Custer's Libbie*, Frost argues that critics like Colonel Samuel D. Sturgis and Captain Frederick W. Benteen soon joined Grant. As many years passed, contemporary critical authors E. A. Brininstool, Charles Brill, Fred Dustin, and Frederic F. Van De Water also emerged prior to Libbie's death. "Dustin called it 'a conspiracy of silence.' Nonsense," writes Frost. "They were as silent as a sonic boom. There is no evidence to support the statement that there was a tacit agreement to wait until Libbie passed on before opening an attack on the General."[26]

Before taking on the crusade of preserving her husband's memory, however, Libbie oversaw George's reburial in the national cemetery at the United States Military Academy at West Point on 10 October 1877.[27] That story began on the Little Big Horn battlefield on 27 June 1876.

Two days after the fighting, Lieutenant James H. Bradley, chief of scouts for the Seventh United States Infantry, and his men came upon the bodies of Custer and his troopers. Bradley, perhaps the first white man to gaze on the carnage along the Little Big Horn, called it an "appalling sight . . . his entire command in the embrace of death."[28] The following day, the Seventh Cavalry buried its dead amid what Lieutenant Edward S. Godfrey called "a scene of sickening, ghastly horror." The bodies of all 209 men who had ridden into the fight with Custer were scattered over the sagebrush-covered ridges and coulees. Most were naked, bloated, and discolored; many had been terribly mutilated. Captain Clifford described the sight as "horrible in the extreme. . . . Here a hand gone, here a foot or a head, gaudy gashes cut in all parts of the body, eyes gouged out, noses and ears cut off, and skulls crushed in."[29]

After coming to Custer's body, Bradley described his wounds as "scarcely discoverable" and he appeared to have died "a natural death." To Bradley, Custer's "expression was rather that of a man who had fallen asleep and enjoyed peaceful dreams than that of one who had met his death amid such fearful scenes as that field had witnessed, the features being wholly without ghastliness or an impress of fear, horror, or despair." During Custer's burial on 28 June, Bradley remembered how others commented on Custer's appearance. "He had died as he had lived — a hero — and excited the remark of those who had known him and saw him there, 'You could almost imagine him standing before you!' "[30] After laying in the hot Montana sun for three days, Custer's body would have been more ghastly than Bradley and others were willing to express in that Victorian era. The living soldiers buried Custer and the other dead during the next two days.

Not surprisingly, the burial details found the task of identifying the dead nearly impossible. Their wounds and postmortem mutilation by the Lakotas and Cheyennes, along with the bloating and decomposition, made their identification even more difficult. Each of the fallen was buried near where he had been killed, the historical record suggests, but a lack of proper tools meant that most men were thinly covered with dirt at best. Few of the crude stakes erected over the hastily dug graves bore names of the dead troopers.

An exception was made for Custer. John Ryan, now the first sergeant of Company M that had fought with Reno, claimed he led a detachment that buried many of the troopers who had fallen around Custer on Last Stand Hill, including his younger brother Captain Tom Custer and his adjutant Lieutenant W. W. Cooke. His lengthy account details the condition of their bodies and the burials. "Gen. Custer was not scalped. He had two bullet wounds—one through his head from one side to the other, another through his body," he recorded. "We found those bodies on a little gravelly knoll surrounded by quite a few bodies of other men. We dug a grave about 18 inches deep and put the General in." He continued, "We then found another body. We could not tell who it was because it was terribly mutilated. Some thought it was Capt. Custer and others differed." The postmortem mutilation of Tom Custer's body specifically caused this debate. "Capt. Custer's head was crushed in as flat as a man's hand," he noted. "He was slit down through the center of his body and also through the muscles of both arms, also slit down through both thighs and disfigured in other ways."

The younger Custer had been the lieutenant of Ryan's Company M for four years before he, as a captain, was assigned as commander of Company C. Because of this previous association, Ryan knew that Tom Custer had the initials T.W.C. marked on his arm with India ink. "We examined the body thoroughly," Ryan wrote, "and we found the letters T.W.C. and that settled it."

Ryan's men laid George and Tom Custer in the same grave, covered them over with pieces of tents and blankets, and mounded them over with dirt. "We found an Indian travois and turned it upside down over the grave and we spiked it down with wooded pins." The contingent then "laid stones around it to keep the wolves from digging them up.

That was the best burial that I saw of any of the bodies on the field," Ryan said.[31]

Ryan's description of the Custers' burial as the "best" on the field is important. That effort should have ensured their easy recovery later. It proved untrue when a military reburial party, commanded by Captain Michael V. Sheridan, returned to the field to recover the bodies of Custer and his officers in June 1877. Despite the apparent care of Ryan's detail the year before, Sheridan's men could not readily identify Custer's body. Wind and rain eroded many of the graves and the markers had been scattered. After a year, the remains were mostly skeletonized as well. The detachments eventually exhumed ten skeletons, including one they believed was Custer's. They also recovered the bodies of Custer's youngest brother, Boston, and his nephew, Autie Reed, which were sent to Michigan for burial. Still, many students of the battle question whether Sheridan's party properly reclaimed Custer's body for reburial at West Point later that fall.

In the 1989 book *Archaeological Perspectives on the Battle of the Little Big Horn*, the authors, Douglas D. Scott, Richard A. Fox, Melissa A. Connor, and Dick Harmon, questioned whether the exhumed remains matched those of the officers and civilians under whose names they had been buried, in part, because of the condition of the corpses. After the battle, some men likely were incorrectly identified. To add to this uncertainty, the exhumation teams had obvious difficulties finding the burial plots.

Scott, Fox, Connor, and Harmon note that after the reburial team removed the skeleton they believed to be Custer's, a rotting uniform shirt with the remains carried the name of one of the regiment's corporals. "Baffled, the searchers then opened a second grave near the first." This nearby grave contained "only a skull, rib cage and femur. For one reason or another—possibly because there was no evidence to the contrary—the searchers were satisfied these bones [from the second grave] were those of Custer."

Some of the recovery team members expressed doubts about this identification. One reportedly said, "It was a disconcerting discovery to find that even the General could not be satisfactorily identified." The Custer brothers' recovery should not have caused so many problems. The four archaeologists suggest that such an internment as Ryan described should have been sufficient to protect the bodies from the elements and animal scavengers. "One would expect, therefore, that the exhumation team would have found two complete sets of remains instead of a single partial skeleton," they argue. "It also seems strange that they apparently found no remnants of the blankets and canvas sheets used to cover the bodies."[32]

With Custer now considered a national hero and his legend already blossoming, Michael Sheridan needed to return with a body, and so he did. The right body? Perhaps not. "There exists the possibility, at least," the archaeologists conclude, "that one or more unknown troopers may be perpetually doomed to the commission of that most cardinal of military sins: impersonating an officer." If so, the bones of one or more of the officers or of Custer's civilian kinsmen may lie either commingled with those of the enlisted men in the common grave under the granite monument on Last Stand Hill or in a solitary grave in Custer National Cemetery itself.[33]

Other experts have also voiced their doubts about Custer's reinternment to the news media. The forensic anthropologist Clyde Snow, who worked with Scott and the other archaeologists on the battlefield digs in the 1980s, told the Associated Press in 1991, "I have a suspicion they got the wrong body." Snow, who studied the records of Custer's burial and exhumation, added, "It would be ironic if some buck private were buried up there at West Point."[34]

On her death in 1933, Libbie was buried beside her husband. The late Douglas McChristian, chief historian at Little Bighorn Battlefield National Monument in 1991, said, "I've often thought in my own warped way that Libbie was sure surprised if there was some corporal lying beside her."[35] Snow also believed, "The thought that it might not be Custer is too delicious to put to rest." If someone other than George Custer were buried there, "they'd probably put the poor guy out somewhere."

The question of whose remains are in Custer's grave may never be answered. Snow suggested, "The only way to put those suspicions to bed would be to look at the bones interred at West Point and see how they gibe with information we have on General Custer." At the time, Snow said that, from a professional standpoint, he would like to dig Custer up and try to identify the remains. As someone who enjoyed myths, however, he preferred maintaining the mystery about the occupant of Custer's burial plot.

Scott also pointed out that the Sheridan detachment's haphazard recovery of Custer's body did not surprise him, as such carelessness was typical of the times. A century or more ago, a tomb or monument to honor the dead was more important than preserving the actual remains. "In the cultural context of the day, the attitude about dying was to memorialize the death rather than worry about the corpus itself," he said. "Their attitude was to go for a skull, maybe some ribs, an arm or a leg, and that was enough."[36]

Right or wrong, Sheridan had a body that he reported was Custer's. On his return to Fort Abraham Lincoln, he telegraphed Libbie Custer for further instructions about burying the ex-general. Wanting her husband buried at West Point, Libbie conferred with Major General John H. Schofield, the academy's commandant. She wrote Sheridan that she had arranged for the burial service to be delayed until October or November "as there will then be a full corps of cadets and officers at West Point and [Schofield] can be better able to pay the honor he wishes to the heroic dead." In the interim, the "sacred dust" was placed in a receiving vault at Poughkeepsie in early August under the care of Philip Hamilton, the father of Captain Louis M. Hamilton who had been killed at the Battle of the Washita in November 1868.

The funeral—full of military pomp—was held on Wednesday, 10 October 1877. The *New York Herald* reported, "A large concourse of people" attended the service.[37] The *New York Times* said, "From every city, town and hamlet on the Hudson people came to participate in the last, sad rites due so brave a soldier." The article added that "the morning had been gloomy, a dense fog enveloping everything. . . . Soon the sun broke through the clouds, the fog lifted, and a cool northerly breeze swept through the valleys."[38]

According to the newspapers, the funeral procession at Poughkeepsie formed at 9:00 AM and included a platoon of police, the Twenty-first New York Regimental Band, Brigadier General George Parker and his staff, a battalion of the Twenty-first New York Infantry Regiment, cadets of the Poughkeepsie Military Institute, the Bald Eagle Artillery Battery, and local clergy. The hearse, drawn by four coal-black horses, was decorated with flags and black crepe. The metallic casket was draped with the same flag that reportedly covered Captain Hamilton's coffin as well. A single floral arrangement, formed into a major general's shoulder strap of two feet long by eight inches wide with a background woven of geraniums and the stars of tube roses, adorned the casket's head. The array signified Custer's volunteer rank during the Civil War.[39]

By 10:30 AM, Custer's body was placed in the ladies saloon aboard the steamer *Mary Powell*. As the boat approached the south dock at West Point, two other steamers, the *Hopkins* and *Henry Smith*, appeared, bearing other civilian and military dignitaries. A detachment of cavalry escorted the casket to the chapel for the services which began at 2:15 PM. Custer's formal uniform helmet and saber were placed on the coffin. At its foot was a beautiful wreath encircling the words "Seventh Cavalry."[40]

The service was brief. Reverend John Forsythe, West

Point's chaplain, read part of the Episcopal burial service and a choir of cadets chanted the Thirty-ninth and Ninetieth Psalms. Among those present, according to the newspapers, were Libbie and Emanuel Custer, Lawrence Barrett's wife Mary, Schofield, and other family and friends. Outside the chapel, the West Point cadets lined up on one side of the roadway, while other military organizations formed on the opposite side. "Mrs. Custer, leaning upon the arm of General Schofield," the *Times* reported, "followed the remains closely, and was deeply affected, shedding tears freely, as did General Custer's father and sister."[41]

A lengthy military procession escorted the remains to the cemetery on the north post overlooking the Hudson River while the band played the funeral march. At the grave the balance of the burial service was read. "Here the body was lowered into its last resting place, earth was sprinkled upon it," the *Times* stated.[42] The corps of cadets fired a three-volley salute. *Harper's Weekly* reported, "The echoes reverberated from side to side of the river, flung back from cliff to cliff, and died mournfully away. The funeral services were over, and the body of the brave Custer was left to rest where his comrades had laid him." By 4:00 PM, the ceremonies ended.[43]

Almost immediately, Libbie Custer began her work of protecting the legacy and reputation of her late spouse. When her husband's life and military career proved to be a highly salable topic for books, she decided to address those subjects herself. Between 1885 and 1890, she wrote three best-selling books—*Boots and Saddles*, *Tenting on the Plains*, and *Following the Guidon*—that remain in print today. Developing a much more comfortable lifestyle, she became a popular speaker and traveled widely.

Louise Barnett points out that Libbie Custer saw her writing task as uplifting the reputation of her late husband. Ironically, since their publication, the books are more often seen as enlightening the public more about her than George.[44]

She never remarried nor did she ever visit the place where George fell in battle, even declining to attend the huge celebration held there on the battle's fiftieth anniversary in June 1926.

Almost seven years later, on 6 April 1933, two days short of her ninety-first birthday, Libbie Custer died in New York City, where she had moved about a year after George's death. A few days later, she was buried next to him in the cemetery at West Point. An obituary noted, "With the death of Mrs. Elizabeth Custer, the West loses one of its last links between the era of her late warrior-husband and the late Gen. George A. Custer loses his most steadfast champion."[45]

Historians Lawrence Frost and John M. Carroll may well have picked up the torch from Libbie as champions for George Custer. Carroll often stated at meetings of the Little Big Horn Associates that Custer aspired to become a national hero. "My every thought was ambitious," Custer stated at one point. "I desired to link my name with acts and men, and in such a manner as to be a mark of honor, not only to the present, but to future generations."[46] In the minds of Libbie Custer, Frost, and Carroll, he certainly achieved that. The rest of us are still trying to untangle that story and figure out how to position George Custer in American history.

Despite Libbie Custer's fight to ensure her husband's positive legacy, detractors tried to bring him down. According to the historic record, only one Seventh Cavalry officer, Captain Frederick W. Benteen, held a cranky attitude about Custer. Among the officers, only a dozen who participated in the Battle of the Washita remained assigned to the regiment in 1876. Six of them are generally classified as Custer supporters—Captains Myles Moylan, Thomas Weir, Tom Custer, George Yates, Myles Keogh, and Lieutenant W. W. Cooke. Five of those six had no opportunity to influence the post-Little Big Horn spin. Tom Custer, Keogh, Yates, and Cooke all died in Montana, while Weir passed away six months later. Only Moylan proved long-lived.

Two other officers at the Washita, Lieutenant James Bell and Captain Owen Hale, were on leave in 1876. Four others participated at the Washita and survived the Little Big Horn—Lieutenants Francis Gibson, Edward Godfrey, Edward Mathey, and Benteen. Only Benteen became renowned for his stinging criticisms of Custer. Godfrey, who lived until 1932, probably influenced the Little Big Horn story more than Benteen through his public statements, his life-long friendship with Libbie Custer, and his own writings.

If any factionalism existed in the Seventh Cavalry in the 1870s, it more likely resulted from military conditions inherent in frontier duty and to common problems in the army during that period. So why has history focused on the Elliott episode at the Battle of the Washita for its presumed long-term effects? The easiest response centers on Custer's own controversial persona. Today, viewing Custer in hindsight, many historians and students of popular culture tend to condemn him for what they consider were his unwarranted attacks on the peaceful Indian villages of 1868 and 1876, with many making him a sidekick of the hated Colonel John M. Chivington, architect of the Sand Creek Massacre of 1864 in Colorado Territory.

When discussing Custer's role in Elliott's demise, writers label him as either a great military hero or as an egotistical gloryhound. For his supporters, Custer never would have willingly abandoned a subordinate officer and the latter's detachment to slaughter in their fight with the Cheyennes. For his detractors, Custer is the scoundrel who sacrificed his subordinate in callous fashion during a massacre of American Indians.

The blame for the Elliott controversy itself more properly falls on Benteen. Within months of the Washita, Benteen published a letter critical of Custer's actions that aggravated the situation, permanently damaging any hopes that a cordial relationship could exist between Custer and his mercurial captain. These issues surrounding Elliott's death primarily existed in Benteen's head. In his later years and as he stumbled in his own career, Benteen, driven by jealousy and anger, sought to demean Custer as much as possible. In the aftermath of the Washita, Custer also failed to bestow public honors on members of his command. To Benteen, a man easily hurt, that oversight was an insult. As author Larry Sklenar notes, "When Custer slighted Benteen, and accepted praise for himself, he made an enemy."[47]

Barnett offered similar observations. Benteen was obsessed with his hatred of Custer until his own death, she believes. The bulk of his most virulent condemnation occurred during the 1890s, his own final years and almost two decades after Custer's death. "Benteen's sense of Custer's overvaluation continued to grate on his equally strong belief in his own undervaluation," she writes. "Although there was no monstrous and demonstrable wrong to explain Benteen's vicious and enduring hatred, the clash of personalities within the confined space of a cavalry regiment, aggravated by petty irritations and a disposition to be envious, may be enough to account for it."[48]

Custer's role in the Washita campaign remains much debated today, especially whether he was a hero or a maniac bent on genocide. In more recent years, some historians have somewhat relaxed their views about Custer's degree of responsibility, seeing him merely as another white man of his times. According to author T. J. Stiles, the *New York Times* in 1868 "fiercely defended" Custer against the charge that he had massacred peaceful Southern Cheyennes. Stiles further notes that Custer's action may have killed a known Cheyenne peace advocate but did not show "unusual carelessness." An Indian war party's trail brought Custer to Black Kettle's doorstep. Custer likely was unaware of whose village he was charging into, but it little mattered. No competent army officer would have risked the advantage of surprise against an expected enemy to verify the latter's identity.[49]

Historian Jerome A. Greene elaborates on the debates

over the Washita, including discussing what would have qualified as a massacre in 1868. He acknowledges that to the Cheyennes, Custer's attack, in the wake of the Sand Creek Massacre just four years before, must have appeared brutal. Greene concludes, however, that the Washita differed significantly from Sand Creek. "Most notably, it was not an indiscriminate slaughter," even though a number of noncombatants may have died in the fighting.[50] At the same time, he notes, for the Cheyennes recalling Sand Creek, the semantical difference between battle and massacre mattered little.

Stiles labels Custer as "unusually bloodthirsty" but states that that fact is less important than that the Indian wars were "unjustifiable."[51] Such criticism of Custer is faulty. Custer was an army officer, who was expected to fight in the defense of his country. In that way, he was no different from such men as Grant or General Dwight D. Eisenhower, both of whom understood, as did Custer, that in war good men die. He was no more bloodthirsty, if at all, than most American army officers who served alongside him in the Civil War as well as those in subsequent American wars.

Many modern critics approach their studies of Custer as if he could have known what he needed to do in his remaining years to assure that he would be remembered as a genius on the battlefield. Much of that thinking is based on what psychiatrist James S. Brust calls hindsight bias over his final events. He notes that this mindset is a weakness common to workers in many fields, including history. Students of history already know how the events they are studying turned out, making them quite susceptible to bias in hindsight. As Brust states, "Events have been analyzed, motivations speculated on, and courses of action guessed and second guessed. All of this has been done from a vantage point that no one had in the field on June 25, 1876." He also points out that Custer had no desire to die at the battle. "Any one of us today could have told him how to avoid defeat at the Little Big Horn. However," he argues, "our well meaning advice to

Custer's ghost contains one important piece of information about the battle that he did not possess—the outcome."[52] Involved as he was in them, Custer himself never had an opportunity to study what he might have done differently for any of those three events in which he participated between 1873 and 1876.

Today, many people often express a view that Custer's goal on 25 June 1876 was part of the overall scheme of white Americans to eliminate American Indians. Custer never expressed such an idea, however. If that were his goal, at some moment in the fighting, the looming outcome of the battle must certainly have been a profound surprise to the ambitious army officer.

In life, Custer viewed himself as a fighter, a task that he certainly enjoyed during the Civil War and on the Great Plains. As a soldier, George Custer understood what his country asked of him. He was an imperfect man asked to take on terribly dangerous challenges on the nation's battlefields. Time after time, he came home to his family and later to his wife. On 25 June 1876, the guns went silent for Custer. Eleven days later at Fort Abraham Lincoln, Libbie Custer shivered, despite the morning heat. Her warrior husband was gone, having given his life for his country.

Notes

PREFACE

1. I will generally rely on the term Lakota in referring to the Sioux. I am following the lead of Richard G. Hardorff, who explained in his book that Sioux is considered derogatory by the Lakotas. Sioux came from a non-Lakota word that identified them as an enemy nation. Hardorff also notes that the use of Lakota has increased in popularity (*Hokahey! A Good Day to Die!: The Indian Casualties of the Custer Fight* [Spokane, Wash.: Arthur H. Clark Co., 1993], p. 14).

2. James S. Robbins, *The Real Custer: From Boy General to Tragic Hero* (Washington, D.C.: Regenery Publishing, 2014), pp. xi–xii.

3. Ibid., p. xvi.

4. Louise Barnett, *Touched By Fire: The Life, Death, and Mythic Afterlife of George Armstrong Custer* (New York: Henry Holt & Co., 1996), p. 30. Historian Edgar I. Stewart, whose book *Custer's Luck* (Norman: University of Oklahoma Press, 1955) remains one of the classic studies on the Battle of the Little Big Horn to this day, noted that Custer's defenders believed any luck Custer enjoyed was "simply the result of downright hard work, unlimited energy, and dauntless courage" (p. 168).

5. For more on Custer and the Michigan Cavalry Brigade and the Third Cavalry Division, *see* Gregory J. W. Urwin, *Custer Victorious: The Civil War Battles of General George Armstrong Custer* (1983; reprint ed., Lincoln: University of Nebraska Press, 1990), and Edward G. Longacre, *Custer and His Wolverines: The Michigan Cavalry Brigade, 1861–1865* (Conshohocken, Pa.: Combined Publishing, 1997).

6. Douglas D. Scott, P. Willey, and Melissa A. Connor, *They Died with Custer: Soldiers' Bones from the Battle of the Little Big Horn* (Norman: University of Oklahoma Press, 1998), pp. 90–93.

7. Greg Toppo and Paul Overberg, *Shreveport (La.) Times*, 1 Nov. 2014, shreveporttimes.com/story/news/local/2014/11/01/changing -face-america-diversity-reshapes-nation/18359819/, accessed 5 Jan. 2019.

CHAPTER 1: EARLY LIFE

1. Emanuel Custer was born on 10 December 1806 in Cresaptown, Maryland, and died on 17 November 1892, in Monroe, Michigan. Maria Custer was born on 31 May 1807 in New Rumley, Ohio, and died on 13 January 1882 in Monroe. Charles B. Wallace, *Custer's Ohio Boyhood: A Brief Account of the Early Life of Major General George Armstrong Custer* (Cadiz, Ohio: Harrison County Historical Society, 1993), p. 13; Sandy Barnard, *Shovels & Speculation: Archaeology Hunts Custer* (Terre Haute, Ind.: AST Press, 1990), p. 54.

2. Barnard, *Shovels & Speculation*, p. 54.

3. Jeffry D. Wert, *Custer: The Controversial Life of George Armstrong Custer* (New York: Simon & Schuster, 1996), p. 15. Emanuel's first name varies in many sources, sometimes appearing with one "m" and at times with two. For the sake of consistency, I will use the one "m" form.

4. Details about Custer's family and life in New Rumley, Ohio, come from Wallace, *Custer's Ohio Boyhood*; Barnard, *Shovels & Speculation*; and Lawrence A. Frost, *The Custer Album* (Seattle: Superior Publishing, 1964). On 7 March 1872, twenty-year-old Margaret Custer married an officer in the Seventh United States Cavalry, twenty-six-year-old Lieutenant James Calhoun, in Monroe. On 25 June 1876, Calhoun died alongside George, Thomas, and Boston Custer. Margaret later remarried John H. Maugham in 1904 (Frost, *General Custer's Libbie* [Seattle, Wash.: Superior Publishing, 1976], p. 200).

5. Louise Barnett, *Touched by Fire: The Life, Death, and Mythic Afterlife of George Armstrong Custer* (New York: Henry Holt & Co., 1996), p. 10.

6. Nevin Custer, "Custer as His Brother Remembers Him," June 1910, newspaper clipping, Lawrence A. Frost Collection, Monroe County Public Library, Monroe, Mich.

7. Wert, *Custer*, p. 18.

8. Robert M. Utley, *Cavalier in Buckskin: George Armstrong Custer and the Western Military Frontier* (Norman: University of Oklahoma Press, 1988), p. 14.

9. Custer, "Custer as His Brother Remembers Him."

10. Emanuel to Elizabeth Bacon Custer, 3 Feb. 1887, in Elizabeth Bacon Custer, *Tenting on the Plains: Or, General Custer in Kansas and Texas* (New York: Charles L. Webster, 1887), pp. 287, 290.

11. Milton Ronsheim, *The Life of General Custer* (Monroe, Mich.: Monroe County Public Library System, 1978), p. 1.

12. Custer, "Custer as His Brother Remembers Him."

13. Ibid.

14. Frederick Whittaker first reported this story in his early biography of Custer, which was rushed into print barely six months after the general's death. Whittaker, *A Complete Life of General George A. Custer*, 2 vols. (1876; reprint ed., Lincoln: University of Nebraska Press, 1993), 1:6. Historian Gregory J. W. Urwin, in his introduction to volume one of the reprint, notes that the book's release spawned the phenomenon known as the "Custer Myth." He added that Whittaker's writing, more than any other print work, "laid the groundwork for the passionate debate that continues to rage over America's most famous frontier soldier and his unforgettable defeat at the Little Big Horn" (pp. xiii–xiv).

15. Quoted in Henry Howe, "A Talk with John Giles of Scio," *Historical Collections of Ohio*, 3 vols. (Columbus, Ohio: Henry Howe & Son, 1891), 1:896–901. According to Howe, he conducted the interview in 1886 when Giles was about seventy years old. Giles was born on 19 January 1818 in Indiana County, Pennsylvania, and died on 9 July 1889 in Conotton, Ohio. He had enlisted in Company A, 126th Ohio Volunteer Infantry Regiment, in August 1862 and served until 25 June 1865, reaching the rank of corporal (John Giles, Grave Registration Card, Harrison County, Ohio, Fold3.com, accessed 21 Feb. 2018). Giles claimed that Custer visited him in his army camp during the Civil War. When Giles protested that a general should not be stopping to see a common soldier, Custer replied, "I thought you knew me better, that I was above all such nonsense as that, especially with an old friend, and the friend of my father." Custer added, "I expect the old man is the same *darned old Copperhead* yet, aint he?" (Howe, "A Talk with John Giles," p. 900).

16. Wallace, *Custer's Ohio Boyhood*, pp. 9, 11; Wert, *Custer*, p. 19.

17. French-Canadian trappers established Frenchtown—later renamed Monroe after President James Monroe visited in 1817—as a trading post along the western shore of Lake Erie near the mouth of the River Raisin. During the War of 1812, British troops and their Indian allies massacred a force of Kentucky riflemen along the river in 1813. By 1852, Monroe had about forty-two hundred residents. The Reeds may have lived at Fifth and Monroe streets and David Reed

likely ran a drayage business. For more about Monroe's history, *see* Frost, *General Custer's Libbie*, pp. 13–18.

18. Frost, "Foreword," in Ronsheim, *Life of General Custer*, n.p.

19. Frost, *General Custer's Libbie*, p. 21.

20. Wert, *Custer*, p. 21.

21. Frost, *The Custer Album: A Pictorial Biography of George Armstrong Custer* (Norman: University of Oklahoma Press, 1990), p. 19.

22. Frost describes Bacon, the town's lone judge, as "a man of means and position," with ties to the legal profession, railroads, banking, and politics. "In short," according to Frost, "he was a man of character and standing in the community." Libbie was his only child (Frost, *Custer Album*, p. 20).

23. Ronsheim, *Life of General Custer*, p. 3; Custer, "Custer as His Brother Remembers Him."

24. Wallace, *Custer's Ohio Boyhood*, p. 64.

25. Barnett, *Touched by Fire*, p. 13.

26. Cadets left West Point for numerous reasons, including academic struggles, physical limitations, or a growing disinterest in a military career. Historian James S. Robbins puts another twist on Custer's class standing. At the time of Abraham Lincoln's victory in the election of 1860, which caused numerous Southern cadets to run for the academy's gates, 87 of the 278 enrolled cadets were from states that seceded. According to Robbins, sixty-five left or were discharged for reasons connected to the Civil War. Six departed for other reasons and fifteen remained with the United States Army (*The Real Custer: From Boy General to Tragic Hero* [Washington, D.C.: Regenery Publishing, 2014], p. 35).

27. Wert, *Custer*, p. 26.

28. Ibid., pp. 26–27.

29. Utley, *Cavalier in Buckskin*, p. 15.

30. Catherine S. Crary, *Dear Belle: Letters from a Cadet and Officer to his Sweetheart, 1858–1865* (Middletown, Conn.: Wesleyan University Press, 1965), p. 41.

31. Utley, *Cavalier in Buckskin*, p. 15.

32. Ibid.

33. Wert, *Custer*, p. 27.

34. Barnett, *Touched by Fire*, p. 16.

35. Wert, *Custer*, p. 29.

CHAPTER 2: THE CIVIL WAR

1. George A. Custer, "War Memoirs," *Galaxy* 21 (June 1876): 811.

2. Ibid., p. 814.

3. Ibid., p. 815.

4. Kearny first obtained a commission as a second lieutenant in the First United States Dragoons commanded by his uncle, Stephen Watts Kearny, in 1837, but resigned in 1846. A month later, he returned to the army at the outbreak of the war with Mexico, raising a company for the First Dragoons. In 1852, he again resigned his commission and joined French forces in Africa. The outbreak of the Civil War brought him back to the United States. By April 1862, he was commanding the Third Division of the Army of the Potomac's III Corps. On 1 September 1862, as Union troops retreated back to Washington, D.C., after their defeat at Second Bull Run, they clashed with Rebels under General Thomas J. ("Stonewall") Jackson at Chantilly, Virginia, in a driving thunderstorm. During the fight, Kearny, on horseback, encountered a Confederate regiment that demanded his surrender. As he turned to escape, the Rebels fired and a Minié ball instantly killed him (David A. Welker, *Tempest at Ox Hill: The Battle of Chantilly* [Cambridge, Mass.: Da Capo Press, 2002], pp. 185–87).

5. Custer, "War Memoirs," p. 815.

6. *See* Lawrence A. Kreiser, Jr., "The Army of the Potomac," *Essential Civil War Curriculum*, essentialcivilwarcurriculum.com/the -army-of-the-potomac.html, accessed 1 Dec. 2020; Stephen W. Sears, *To the Gates of Richmond: The Peninsula Campaign* (New York: Ticknor & Fields, 1992).

7. Moses A. Luce, "Custer's First Battle by One Who Took Part in It as a Member of the Fourth Michigan," *Overland Monthly and Out West Magazine* 31 (Jan.–June 1898): 280–81.

8. Ibid., p. 281. Luce states that Captain James W. Forsyth of the Eighteenth United States Infantry Regiment also accompanied the Union troopers. Known primarily as a staff officer, Forsyth later became a cavalry commander on the Great Plains. He is best remembered as the commander of the Seventh Cavalry when its soldiers surrounded and fired on Big Foot's Lakota band at Wounded Knee, South Dakota, on 29 December 1890.

9. George B. McClellan, *McClellan's Own Story: The War for the Union* (New York: Charles L. Webster, 1887), p. 364.

10. Elizabeth Bacon Custer, *The Civil War Memories of Elizabeth Bacon Custer*, ed. Arlene Reynolds (Austin: University of Texas Press, 1994), p. 74.

11. McClellan, *McClellan's Own Story*, p. 365.

12. Gregory J. W. Urwin, *Custer Victorious: The Civil War Battles of General George Armstrong Custer* (1983; reprint ed., Lincoln: University of Nebraska Press, 1990), pp. 48–49.

13. Custer, *Civil War Memories*, pp. 4–6.

14. Ibid., pp. 5–7; Jeffry D. Wert, *Custer: The Controversial Life of George Armstrong Custer* (New York: Simon & Schuster, 1996), pp. 61–70, 122–24.

15. Wert, *Custer*, pp. 66–72.

16. Urwin, *Custer Victorious*, pp. 55–59; Wert, *Custer*, pp. 80–83.

17. For the background on the regiments in the Michigan Cavalry Brigade, I have relied on James Henry Avery, *Under Custer's Command: The Civil War Journal of James Henry Avery*, comp. Karla Jean Husby, ed. Eric Wittenberg (Washington, D.C.: Brassey's, 2000); Robert F. O'Neill, *Chasing Jeb Stuart and John Mosby: The Union Cavalry in Northern Virginia from Second Manassas to Gettysburg* (Jefferson, N.C.: McFarland, 2012); and Charles H. Safford, *I Rode With Custer: The Civil War Diary of Charles H. Safford, Brevet Major, 5th Michigan Cavalry*, ed. Paul Davis (Detroit, Mich.: Aston Z. Publishing, 2014).

18. Joseph T. Copeland (6 May 1813–6 May 1893) was a highly placed figure in antebellum Michigan politics and served as a justice on the Michigan Supreme Court from 1852 to 1857. Initially, Copeland served as the lieutenant colonel and commander of the First Michigan Cavalry Regiment and then the Fifth Michigan Cavalry. After Custer replaced him as leader of the Michigan Cavalry Brigade, he handled mostly administrative assignments, including commanding a depot for drafted men at Annapolis, Maryland, and later Pittsburgh, Pennsylvania. He also commanded a military prison at Alton, Illinois, until his resignation on 8 November 1865 ("Joseph T. Copeland," Michigan Supreme Court Historical Society, micourthistory.org/justices/joseph-copeland, accessed 17 Aug. 2020).

19. Urwin, *Custer Victorious*, pp. 67–68; O'Neill, *Chasing Jeb Stuart and John Mosby*, pp. 18–26.

20. Urwin, *Custer Victorious*, p. 67.

21. John Singleton Mosby (6 Dec. 1833–30 May 1916), nicknamed

the "Gray Ghost," was commander of the Forty-third Battalion of the First Virginia Cavalry, also referred to as Mosby's Rangers or Mosby's Raiders. His partisan rangers were known for their lightning quick raids and ability to elude Union pursuers by blending in with local civilians. Major books written about Mosby include Virgil Carrington Jones, *Ranger Mosby* (Chapel Hill: University of North Carolina Press, 1944) and Wert, *Mosby's Rangers: The True Adventures of the Most Famous Command of the Civil War* (New York: Simon & Schuster, 1990).

22. George Gordon Meade (31 Dec. 1815–6 Nov. 1872) was a career army officer, who had been a division and then corps commander in the Army of the Potomac before becoming its leader. *See* Allen C. Guelzo, *Gettysburg: The Last Invasion* (New York: Alfred A. Knopf, 2013), pp. 85–88.

23. Urwin, *Custer Victorious*, pp. 63–69.

24. Paul R. Gorman, "J. E. B. Stuart and Gettysburg," *Gettysburg Magazine* (July 1989), p. 89.

25. Paul M. Shevchuk, "The Battle of Hunterstown, Pennsylvania, July 2, 1863," ibid., p. 93.

26. Ibid., pp. 93–94; Guelzo, *Gettysburg*, pp. 359–60.

27. Edward G. Longacre, *Custer and His Wolverines: The Michigan Cavalry Brigade, 1861–1865* (Cambridge, Mass.: Da Capo Press, 1997), p. 138.

28. Shevchuk, "Battle of Hunterstown," pp. 93–96.

29. Guelzo, *Gettysburg*, pp. 360–61.

30. Shevchuk, "Battle of Hunterstown," p. 96.

31. Ibid., pp. 93–96.

32. Urwin, *Custer Victorious*, p. 70.

33. Ibid., *Custer Victorious*, pp. 70–75.

34. James H. Kidd, *Personal Recollections of a Cavalryman with Custer's Michigan Cavalry Brigade in the Civil War* (Ionia, Mich.: By the Author, 1902), p. 145.

35. Urwin, *Custer Victorious*, pp. 75–77.

36. Steven Gaines to Elizabeth B. Custer, 12 Nov. 1906, Elizabeth Bacon Custer Collection, Little Bighorn Battlefield National Monument, Crow Agency, Mont.

37. Urwin, *Custer Victorious*, pp. 77–78.

38. Kidd to his parents, 9 July 1863, James H. Kidd Papers, Bentley Historical Library, University of Michigan Libraries, Ann Arbor.

39. Charles H. Town (28 May 1828–7 May 1865) was only thirty-six when he died of consumption in Dexter, Michigan. He had enrolled in Company B of the First Michigan Cavalry, as a captain on 8 August 1861 and was promoted to major on 22 August. On 30 September 1862, he succeeded Colonel Thornton F. Brodhead, who died from a mortal wound on 2 September, as the regiment's commander. U.S., Charles H. Town and Thornton F. Brodhead records, *Civil War Soldier Records and Profiles*, ancestry.com.

40. Urwin, *Custer Victorious*, pp. 79–81.

41. George A. Custer to his sister, 26 July 1863, George A. Custer Collection (George Custer Collection), Monroe County Public Library, Monroe, Mich.

42. Urwin, *Custer Victorious*, p. 81. Longacre was less enthusiastic about Custer's role, merely noting that "Custer's Wolverines could claim a heroic share of the credit" (Longacre, *Custer and His Wolverines*, p. 153).

43. Edward G. to Mollie Granger, 3 Sept. 1863, in *An Aide to Custer: The Civil War Letters of Lt. Edward G. Granger*, ed. Sandy Barnard, comp. Thomas E. Singelyn (Norman: University of Oklahoma Press, 2018), pp. 117–19.

44. Urwin, *Custer Victorious*, pp. 96–104.

45. Marguerite Merington, ed., *The Custer Story: The Life and Intimate Letters of General George A. Custer and His Wife Elizabeth* (New York: Devin-Adair, 1950), pp. 84–85.

46. Custer, *Civil War Memories*, p. 35.

47. Ibid., p. 45.

48. Ibid., p. 46.

49. Ron Chernow, *Grant* (New York: Penguin Press, 2017), pp. 337–45.

50. Donald Stoker, *The Grand Design: Strategy and the U.S. Civil War* (New York: Oxford University Press, 2010), pp. 352–53.

51. Chernow, *Grant*, pp. 369–70. Chernow's comparison of the two men is interesting, but Grant certainly benefitted from greater resources, especially as the war dragged on through 1864 into 1865.

52. *Wheeling (W.Va.) Register*, 24 Aug. 1880.

53. Wert, *Custer*, p. 146.

54. Philip H. Sheridan (6 Mar. 1831–5 Aug. 1888) was one of the most celebrated Union generals along with Ulysses S. Grant and William T. Sherman. He graduated from West Point in 1853 and

served on the frontier for eight years. When the Civil War began, he remained a second lieutenant, but over a seven-month period between May and December 1862, he rose from captain to major general of volunteers, eventually becoming a major general in the Regular Army in November 1864. His outstanding performances at the Battles of Chickamauga and Missionary Ridge in September and November 1863 brought him to Grant's attention. After the war, then President Grant promoted Sheridan to lieutenant general. He would play an instrumental role during the later Indian wars, including the Great Sioux War of 1876–1877. In 1884, when Sherman retired, Sheridan became commanding general of the U.S. Army, eventually receiving the full rank of general in June 1888. He died about a month later and was buried in Arlington National Cemetery in Virginia (Ezra J. Warner, *Generals in Blue: Lives of the Union Commanders* [Baton Rouge: Louisiana State University Press, 1989], pp. 437–39).

55. Custer to his sister, 23 Apr. 1864, George Custer Collection.

56. Eric J. Wittenberg, *Glory Enough for All: Sheridan's Second Raid The Battle of Trevillian Station* (Washington, D.C.: Brassey's, 2002), pp. 98–112; Jay Monaghan, "Custer's 'Last Stand'—Trevilian Station, 1864," in *The Custer Reader*, ed. Paul Andrew Hutton (Lincoln: University of Nebraska Press, 1992), pp. 58–59.

57. Wittenberg, *Glory Enough for All*, p. 112.

58. Kidd to John Robertson, Adjutant General of Michigan, 17 Dec. 1864, James H. Kidd Papers, Bentley Historical Library, University of Michigan, Ann Arbor.

59. U.S., Department of War, *The War of the Rebellion: A Compilation of the Official Records of the Union and Confederate Armies*, 70 vols. (Washington, D.C.: Government Printing Office, 1880–1901), ser. 1, vol. 36, pt. 1, p. 824; Merington, *Custer Story*, p. 105.

60. Kidd, *Recollections of a Cavalryman*, pp. 364–65; Urwin, *Custer Victorious*, p. 163.

61. Urwin, *Custer Victorious*, pp. 163–64.

62. Granger to unknown, [13 or 14] June 1864, in *Aide to Custer*, pp. 246–55.

63. Urwin, *Custer Victorious*, p. 169.

64. Scott C. Patchan, "The Battle of Crooked Run: George Custer's Opening Act in the Shenandoah Valley," *North & South* 11 (Dec. 2008): 76–83.

65. Urwin, *Custer Victorious*, p. 174.

66. Patchan, "Battle of Crooked Run," p. 82.

67. Wert, *Custer*, pp. 211–30.

68. Ibid., pp. 228–30.

69. Merington, *Custer Story*, p. 165. Libbie Custer retained Sheridan's gift, which by the terms of her will was given to the national collections housed at the Smithsonian Institution in Washington, D.C. (Urwin, *Custer Victorious*, p. 267).

70. John M. Carroll, *Custer in Texas: An Interrupted Narrative* (New York: Sol Lewis & Liveright, 1975), pp. 7–8.

71. Urwin, *Custer Victorious*, p. 8.

72. Ibid., p. 260.

CHAPTER 3: ON THE CENTRAL AND SOUTHERN PLAINS

1. According to the Official Data Foundation's inflation calculator, Custer's offer of $16,000 from Mexico in 1866 would be the equivalent of $260,730.57 in 2020 (officialdata.org/us/inflation/1866 ?amount=16000). Thus, the offer in 1866 must have been tempting to Custer and his wife.

2. T. J. Stiles, *Custer's Trials: A Life on the Frontier of a New America* (New York: Alfred A. Knopf, 2015), pp. 329–53, 420–28.

3. Robert M. Utley, *Cavalier in Buckskin: George Armstrong Custer and the Western Military Frontier* (Norman: University of Oklahoma Press, 1988), p. 42.

4. Ibid., p. 41; Utley, *Frontier Regulars: The United States Army and the Indian, 1866–1891* (New York: Macmillan, 1973), is also highly recommended for its discussion of Indian life and culture in the post–Civil War period.

5. Herman J. Viola, *Little Bighorn Remembered: The Untold Story of Custer's Last Stand* (New York: Times Books, 1999), p. 14.

6. For more on John Ryan, *see* Sandy Barnard, *Custer's First Sergeant John Ryan* (Terre Haute, Ind.: AST Press, 1996); Barnard, ed., *Ten Years with Custer: A 7th Cavalryman's Memoirs* (Terre Haute, Ind.: AST Press, 2001); and Barnard, ed., *Campaigning with the Irish Brigade: Pvt. John Ryan, 28th Massachusetts* (Terre Haute, Ind.: AST Press, 2001).

7. For further details on Ryan's life, *see* Barnard, *Ten Years with Custer*, pp. 1–8. For more on the typical frontier soldiers, *see* Utley, *Frontier Regulars*, pp. 22–23.

8. Paul L. Hedren, *Great Sioux War Orders of Battle: How the United States Waged War on the Northern Plains, 1876–1877* (Norman, Okla.: Arthur H. Clark Co., 2011), p. 21.

9. Don Rickey, Jr., *Forty Miles a Day on Beans and Hay: The Enlisted Soldier Fighting the Indian Wars* (1963; reprint ed., Norman: University of Oklahoma Press, 1989), p. 18; Barnard, "The Widow Custer, Consolation Comes from Custer's Best Friend," *Greasy Grass* 17 (2001): 2.

10. *See* Jeff Broome, "Custer's Summer Indian Campaign of 1867," *Denver Westerner's Roundup* (July–Aug. 2008): 3–33; Broome, *Custer into the West: With the Journal and Maps of Lieutenant Henry Jackson* (El Segundo, Calif.: Upton & Sons, 2008).

11. Broome, *Custer into the West*, pp. 45–57, 71–78.

12. Ibid., p. 77.

13. Ibid., p. 79; Lawrence A. Frost, *The Court-Martial of General George Armstrong Custer* (Norman: University of Oklahoma Press, 1968), pp. 242–43.

14. Blaine Burkey, *Custer, Come at Once!: The Fort Hays Years of George and Elizabeth Custer, 1867–1870* (Hays, Kans.: Society of Friends of Fort Hays, 1991), p. 30.

15. Frost, *Court-Martial of General George Armstrong Custer*, pp. 99–100.

16. *Leavenworth (Kans.) Daily Conservative*, 19 Jan. 1868, ibid., p. 263.

17. Edward G. to Mollie Granger, 3 Sept. 1863, in *An Aide to Custer: The Civil War Letters of Lt. Edward G. Granger*, ed. Barnard, comp. Thomas E. Singelyn (Norman: University of Oklahoma Press, 2018), pp. 117–19.

18. Sheridan to John A. Rawlins, 15 Apr. 1868, General Correspondence, 1853–1888, Philip H. Sheridan Papers, Library of Congress, Washington, D.C.

19. Utley, *Cavalier in Buckskin*, p. 55.

20. Louise Barnett, *Touched by Fire: The Life, Death, and Mythic Afterlife of George Armstrong Custer* (New York: Henry Holt & Co., 1996), p. 64.

21. Frost, *The Custer Album: A Pictorial Biography of General George A. Custer* (1964; reprint ed., New York: Bonanza Books, 1984), p. 81; Jeffry D. Wert, *Custer: The Controversial Life of George Armstrong Custer* (New York: Simon & Schuster, 1996), p. 264.

22. Utley, *Cavalier in Buckskin*, p. 61.

23. Ibid.

24. Stan Hoig, *The Battle of the Washita* (Lincoln: University of Nebraska Press, 1979), p. 82.

25. Utley, *Cavalier in Buckskin*, p. 61.

26. Utley, *Frontiersmen in Blue: The United States Army and the Indian, 1848–1865* (1967; reprint ed., Lincoln: University of Nebraska Press, 1981), pp. 294–97.

27. Utley, *Cavalier in Buckskin*, p. 64.

28. Utley, *Frontier Regulars*, p. 151.

29. Utley, *Cavalier in Buckskin*, p. 68.

30. Jerome A. Greene, *Washita: The U.S. Army and the Southern Cheyennes, 1867–1869* (Norman: University of Oklahoma Press, 2004), p. 124.

31. Ron Chernow, *Grant* (New York: Penguin Press, 2017), p. 833.

32. Barnard, *A Hoosier Quaker Goes to War: The Life & Death of Major Joel H. Elliott, 7th Cavalry* (Wake Forest, N.C.: AST Press, 2010), p. 32.

33. Richard Hardorff, *Washita Memories: Eyewitness Views of Custer's Attack on Black Kettle's Village* (Norman: University of Oklahoma Press, 2005), p. 32.

34. Ibid.

35. Greene, *Washita*, pp. 174–75.

36. Barnard, *Hoosier Quaker Goes to War*, p. 282.

37. Peter Cozzens, *Eyewitnesses to the Indian Wars, 1865–1890: Conquering the Southern Plains* (Mechanicsburg, Pa.: Stackpole, 2003), p. 348.

38. Barnard, *Ten Years with Custer*, p. 77.

39. Greene, *Washita*, p. 124.

40. Custer, *My Life on the Plains* (1874; reprint ed., Lincoln, Nebr.: Bison Books, 1972), p. 257.

41. Edward S. Godfrey to unknown, n.d., WA-2, File 11 86.01, Box 33, Joseph B. Thoburn Papers, Archives and Manuscript Division, Oklahoma Historical Society, Oklahoma City.

42. Utley, *Cavalier in Buckskin*, p. 75.

43. Ibid., pp. 75–76.

44. William A. Graham, *The Custer Myth: A Source Book of Custeriana* (New York: Bonanza Books, 1953), p. 337.

45. Murphy to Taylor, 4 Dec. 1868, in Barnett, *Touched by Fire*, p. 164.

46. Wynkoop to Taylor, 26 Jan. 1869, ibid., p. 164; Greene, *Washita*, pp. 164–65.

47. Greene, *Washita*, p. 164.

48. Ibid., p. 165.

49. Ibid., pp. 166–67.

50. For more detail on this campaign, *see* Louis Kraft, *Custer and the Cheyenne* (El Segundo, Calif.: Upton & Sons, 1995), pp. 91–178.

51. Custer, *My Life on the Plains*, p. 554.

52. Barnard, *Ten Years with Custer*, p. 90. Ryan relates that Custer was accompanied by his adjutant, Lieutenant Myles Moylan, the regiment's chief trumpeter, and its sergeant major.

53. Morgan was the twenty-four-year-old wife of a farmer, who had been captured in September 1868 during a raid on the Solomon River settlements. White, only seventeen at the time, had been seized in the Republican River valley the previous August in an attack in which her father had been killed. According to Ryan's account, the women were in "pitiful condition" (Barnard, *Ten Years with Custer*, pp. 92–93).

54. Ibid., p. 104. In his later years, Ryan also exchanged frequent correspondence with Libbie Custer, whom he described as "a woman of refined manners and a perfect lady."

55. Sheridan to Custer, 2 Mar. 1869, in *The Custer Story: The Life and Intimate Letters of General Custer and his Wife Elizabeth*, ed. Marguerite Merington (New York: Devin-Adair, 1950), p. 228.

56. *See* Peter Harrison, *Monahsetah* (London: English Westerners Society, 2015).

57. Shirley A. Leckie, *Elizabeth Bacon Custer and the Making of a Myth* (Norman: University of Oklahoma Press, 1993), p. 210.

58. Barnard, *Custer's First Sergeant*, p. 137.

59. Eric Foner, *Reconstruction: America's Unfinished Revolution, 1863–1877* (New York: Harper & Row, 1988), p. 415.

60. For more on the Seventh Cavalry's experience during Reconstruction, *see* Barnard, *Ten Years with Custer*, pp. 133–68, and Andrew H. Myers, "Prelude to the Little Bighorn: The Seventh U.S. Cavalry in the South Carolina Upcountry," in *Recovering the Piedmont Past: Unexplored Moments in Nineteenth-Century Upcountry South*

Carolina History, ed. Timothy P. Grady and Melissa Walker (Columbia: University of South Carolina Press, 2013), pp. 53–86.

61. Numerous works exist on the broad topic of Reconstruction, but only a handful focus on the military aspects that involved the Seventh Cavalry. *See* Barnard, *Ten Years with Custer*, pp. 133–68; J. Michael Martinez, *Carpetbaggers, Cavalry, and the Ku Klux Klan: Exposing the Invisible Empire During Reconstruction* (Lanham, Md.: Rowman & Littlefield, 2007); Jerry L. West, *The Reconstruction Ku Klux Klan in York County, South Carolina, 1865–1877* (Jefferson, N.C.: McFarland, 2002).

CHAPTER 4: ON THE NORTHERN GREAT PLAINS

1. T. J. Stiles, *Custer's Trials: A Life on the Frontier of a New America* (New York: Alfred A. Knopf, 2015), p. 359.

2. Richmond L. Clow, *Spotted Tail: Warrior and Statesman* (Pierre: South Dakota Historical Society Press, 2019), pp. 70–71.

3. Baron N. Schilling to Elizabeth Bacon Custer, 25 Mar. 1877, in Louise Barnett, *Touched by Fire: The Life, Death, and Mythic Afterlife of George Armstrong Custer* (New York: Henry Holt & Co., 1996), p. 216.

4. Stiles, *Custer's Trials*, p. 366.

5. Brian W. Dippie, "Introduction," in *Nomad: George A. Custer in Turf, Field and Farm*, ed. Dippie (Austin: University of Texas Press, 1980), pp. xiii–xvii.

6. Charles W. Larned to *Chicago Inter-Ocean*, 30 Apr. 1873, in "Expedition to the Yellowstone River in 1873: Letters of a Young Cavalry Officer," ed. George Frederick Howe, *The Custer Reader*, ed. Paul Andrew Hutton (Lincoln: University of Nebraska Press, 1992), p. 185.

7. An 1852 graduate of West Point, Stanley was highly experienced in the peacetime and wartime army. During the United States Civil War, he had risen to the rank of major general of volunteers and received the Medal of Honor for his actions during the defense of Franklin, Tennessee, on 30 November 1864. His primary weakness in 1873 was telling: alcoholism.

8. For more on the Yellowstone Expedition of 1873, *see* Lawrence A. Frost, *Custer's 7th Cavalry and the Campaign of 1873* (El Segundo, Calif.: Upton & Sons, 1986); M. John Lubetkin, *Jay Cooke's Gamble: The Northern Pacific Railroad, the Sioux, and the Panic of*

1873 (Norman: University of Oklahoma Press, 2006), pp. 175–266; Lubetkin, ed., *Custer and the 1873 Yellowstone Survey: A Documentary History* (Norman, Okla.: Arthur H. Clark Co., 2013); Robert M. Utley, *Cavalier in Buckskin: George Armstrong Custer and the Western Military Frontier* (Norman: University of Oklahoma Press, 1988), pp. 115–23.

9. Stiles, *Custer's Trials*, pp. 384–85.

10. Utley, *Cavalier in Buckskin*, p. 119.

11. Barnett, *Touched by Fire*, p. 237.

12. Larned to his mother, 11 June 1873, quoted in Lubetkin, *Jay Cooke's Gamble*, pp. 180–81.

13. Stiles, *Custer's Trials*, pp. 378–80.

14. Ibid., p. 395.

15. Utley, *Cavalier in Buckskin*, p. 122.

16. Stiles, *Custer's Trials*, p. 399.

17. Utley, *Cavalier in Buckskin*, p. 126.

18. Lubetkin, *Jay Cooke's Gamble*, p. xv. Lubetkin provides a strong summary of the financial and political events, often behind the scenes, that forced the Battle of the Little Big Horn to occur in 1876.

19. Ibid.

20. Stiles, *Custer's Trials*, p. 406.

21. Max E. Gerber, "The Custer Expedition of 1874: A New Look," *North Dakota History* 40 (Winter 1973): 5.

22. Edward Lazarus, *Black Hills, White Justice: The Sioux Nation Versus the United States, 1775 to the Present* (New York: HarperCollins, 1991), pp. 3–6.

23. Ibid., pp. 5–6.

24. Ibid., p. 7.

25. James S. Robbins, *The Real Custer: From Boy General to Tragic Hero* (Washington, D.C.: Regenery Publishing, 2014), pp. 338–39.

26. *See* Stiles, *Custer's Trials*, pp. 407–40, for an excellent summary of Custer's failures in business and the impact it had on his later life.

27. Terry Mort, *Thieves Road: The Black Hills Betrayal and Custer's Path to Little Bighorn* (Amherst, N.Y.: Prometheus Books, 2015), p. 221.

28. Ibid., p. 223.

29. Ibid., p. 224.

30. Ibid., p. 239.

31. Sandy Barnard, ed., *Ten Years with Custer: A Seventh Cavalryman's Memoirs* (Terre Haute, Ind.: AST Press, 2001), pp. 223–25.

32. Ibid., p. 224.

33. Mort, *Thieves Road*, p. 240.

34. James Calhoun, *With Custer in '74: James Calhoun's Diary of the Black Hills Expedition*, ed. Frost (Provo, Utah: Brigham Young University Press, 1979), p. 60.

35. George A. Custer to Alfred Terry, telegram, 8 Aug. 1875, quoted in Frost, *General Custer's Libbie* (Seattle, Wash.: Superior Publishing, 1975), p. 212.

36. Mort, *Thieves Road*, p. 260.

37. Elizabeth B. Custer, "General Custer and the Indian Chiefs," introduction to Charles Francis Bates, "The Red Man and the Black Hills," *Outlook Magazine* 146 (27 July 1927): 408.

38. Ernest Grafe and Paul Horsted, *Exploring with Custer: The 1874 Black Hills Expedition* (Custer, S.Dak.: Golden Valley Press, 2002), p. xi.

39. Ibid.

40. Donald Jackson, *Custer's Gold: The United States Cavalry Expedition of 1874* (New Haven, Conn.: Yale University Press, 1966), p. 120.

41. Utley, *Frontier Regulars: The United States Army and the Indian, 1866–1891* (New York: Macmillan, 1973), pp. 245–46; Utley, *The Lance and the Shield: The Life and Times of Sitting Bull* (New York: Henry Holt & Co., 1993), pp. 125–27.

42. Utley, *Lance and the Shield*, pp. 127–28.

43. Utley, *Frontier Regulars*, pp. 244–46.

44. For more on Kellogg's role, *see* Barnard, *I Go With Custer: The Life and Death of Reporter Mark Kellogg* (Bismarck, N.Dak.: Bismarck Tribune Publishing, 1996), pp. 92–98.

45. Utley, *Cavalier in Buckskin*, p. 153.

46. Stiles, *Custer's Trials*, pp. 420–22.

47. Ibid., p. 154.

CHAPTER 5: THE BATTLE OF THE LITTLE BIG HORN

1. Michael L. Hedegaard, "Colonel Joseph J. Reynolds and the Saint Patrick's Day Celebration on Powder River: Battle of Powder

River (Montana, 17 March 1876)," (master's thesis, U.S. Army Command and General Staff College, 2001), pp. 8–12.

2. Sandy Barnard, *Photographing Custer's Battlefield: The Images of Kenneth F. Roahen* (Norman: University of Oklahoma Press, 2016), pp. 29–40.

3. For the best account of the Powder River battle, *see* Paul L. Hedren, *Powder River: Disastrous Opening of the Great Sioux War* (Norman: University of Oklahoma Press, 2016).

4. Much of the account of Custer's Little Big Horn Campaign is drawn from James S. Brust, Brian C. Pohanka, and Sandy Barnard, *Where Custer Fell: Photographs of the Little Bighorn Battlefield Then and Now* (Norman: University of Oklahoma Press, 2005), pp. 5–13.

5. Barnard, *I Go With Custer: The Life and Death of Reporter Mark Kellogg* (Bismarck, N.Dak.: Bismarck Tribune Publishing, 1996), pp. 103–4.

6. Robert M. Utley, *Cavalier in Buckskin: George Armstrong Custer and the Western Military Frontier* (Norman: University of Oklahoma Press, 1988), pp. 161–62.

7. Ibid., *Cavalier in Buckskin*, p. 162.

8. Lawrence A. Frost, *General Custer's Libbie* (Seattle, Wash.: Superior Publishing, 1975), pp. 225–26.

9. Alfred H. Terry to Philip H. Sheridan, 16 May 1876, letters received, headquarters, Military Division of the Missouri, Microfilm Publication M1495, Records of the U.S. Army Continental Commands, 1821–1920, Record Group 393, National Archives and Records Administration, Washington, D.C.

10. Michael N. Donahue, *Where the Rivers Ran Red: The Indian Fights of George Armstrong Custer* (Montrose, Colo.: San Juan Publishing, 2018), pp. 134–35.

11. Ibid., p. 135.

12. Ibid., p. 139.

13. Ibid., p. 140.

14. Barnard, *I Go with Custer*, p. 115.

15. *New York Herald*, 11 July 1876.

16. Ibid.

17. Quoted in John S. Gray, *Centennial Campaign: The Sioux War of 1876* (Norman: University of Oklahoma Press, 1988), pp. 147–48.

18. Ibid., p. 287.

19. The actual site of the Crow's Nest remains a hotly debated

subject. For more about this controversy, *see* Barnard, *Photographing Custer's Battlefield*, pp. 43–55.

20. Second Lieutenant Winfield Scott Edgerly wrote to his wife on 4 July, "We were told that the Indians had undoubtedly discovered our presence as several had been seen on the bluffs and the only thing left for us to do was move on them at once . . . now all hopes of a surprise were gone" (George M. Clark, *Scalp Dance: The Edgerly Papers on the Battle of the Little Big Horn* [Oswego, N.Y.: Heritage Press, 1985], p. 24).

21. At the Reno Court of Inquiry, Captain Moylan testified that Reno, Benteen, Keogh, and Yates were given command of battalions, noting, "Each of these battalions I have named consisted of three companies, except Captain Yates' which was two companies" (Moylan, testimony, in *Reno Court of Inquiry: Official Record, Court of Inquiry to Investigate the Conduct of Major Marcus A. Reno, 7th U.S. Cavalry, at the Battle of the Little Big Horn River, Montana, June 25–26, 1876*, ed. Ronald H. Nichols [Crow Agency, Mont.: Custer Battlefield Historical & Museum Association, 1992], p. 213). Edgerly similarly informed researcher Walter M. Camp that Custer divided the regiment "into four battalions, Benteen, Reno, Keogh and Yates and had McDougall rear guard for pack train. He took Keogh and Yates with him" (Camp, interview with Winfield S. Edgerly, in *Custer in '76: Walter Camp's Notes on the Custer Fight*, ed. Kenneth Hammer [Provo, Utah: Brigham Young University Press, 1976], p. 54). While other terminology appears in the literature to denote sub-regimented segments of the command, in *Where Custer Fell*, Brust, Pohanka, and I used the term battalion to describe units of two or more companies. While most battle historians assume Keogh commanded Companies C, I, and L and Yates E and F, the evidence is less than conclusive on that point and subject to interpretation. Earlier in the campaign, Keogh had commanded Companies, B, C, and I and Yates E, F, and L (Brust, Pohanka, and Barnard, *Where Custer Fell*, p. 7).

22. For more on the battle, *see* Hedren, *Powder River*; Zenobia Self, "Court-Martial of J. J. Reynolds," *Military Affairs* 37 (Apr. 1973): 52–56.

23. Gray, *Centennial Campaign*, p. 296. Joe Sills Jr. and Ronald H. Nichols determined the total number of men with Reno as 165, 130

of whom were soldiers. Ronald H. Nichols, *In Custer's Shadow: Major Marcus Reno* (Fort Collins, Colo.: Old Army Press, 1999), p. 184.

24. William A. Graham, *Story of the Little Big Horn: Custer's Last Fight* (New York: Bonanza Books, 1926), p. 249; Daniel A. Knipe, battle account recorded 16–17 June 1908, in *Custer in '76*, pp. 92, 97. In his account to Camp, Daniel Kanipe spells his name differently from his enlistment records that have him listed as "Knipe."

25. John Stands in Timber and Margot Liberty, *Cheyenne Memories* (Lincoln: University of Nebraska Press, 1967), pp. 197–98.

26. Donahue, *Where the Rivers Ran Red*, p. 158.

27. Ibid.; Barnard, *A Hoosier Quaker Goes to War: The Life and Death of Major Joel H. Elliott, 7th Cavalry* (Wake Forest, N.C.: AST Press, 2010), p. 261.

28. Louise Barnett, *Touched by Fire: The Life, Death, and Mythic Afterlife of George Armstrong Custer* (New York: Henry Holt & Co., 1996), pp. 162–63.

29. Brian Pohanka and I frequently discussed this topic during visits to Little Bighorn Battlefield National Monument in the 1990s. For more, *see* Brust, Pohanka, and Barnard, *Where Custer Fell*, p. 46.

30. Gray gives the loss as forty killed, thirteen wounded, and seventeen abandoned in the timber (*Centennial Campaign*, p. 296). Nichols interprets the loss as thirty-seven killed, ten wounded, and seventeen abandoned (*In Custer's Shadow*, p. 383).

31. Donahue, *Where the Rivers Ran Red*, p. 184.

32. Two of the more thought-provoking analyses of the Weir Point episode are Francis B. Taunton, "The Enigma of Weir Point," in *No Pride in the Little Big Horn*, ed. Taunton (London: English Westerners' Society, 1987), pp. 17–41, and Joe Sills, Jr., "Weir Point Perspective," in *7th Annual Symposium, CBHMA, Held at Hardin, Montana, on June 25, 1993* (Hardin, Mont.: Custer Battlefield Historical & Museum Association, 1994), pp. 45–51.

33. Gray gives a total of twelve killed—thirteen, if one includes farrier Vincent Charley who suffered a brutal death near Weir's Point—and forty-one wounded during the two-day siege (*Centennial Campaign*, p. 206). Nichols places the loss at fifteen killed and fifty-five wounded (*In Custer's Shadow*, pp. 384–85). The subsequent deaths from wounds brought the fatalities sustained in the siege to twenty.

34. Numerous studies of the Little Big Horn have been pub-

lished over the years and have been the basis for this summary. *See* Edgar I. Stewart, *Custer's Luck* (Norman: University of Oklahoma Press, 1955); Bruce Liddic, *Vanishing Victory: Custer's Final March* (El Segundo, Calif.: Upton & Sons, 2004); James Donovan, *A Terrible Glory: Custer and the Little Bighorn—the Last Great Battle of the West* (New York: Little, Brown, 2008); Donahue, *Where the Rivers Ran Red*; Gray, *Centennial Campaign*.

35. Graham, *The Custer Myth: A Source Book of Custeriana* (New York: Bonanza Books, 1953), p. 290; John Mitchell, testimony, *Reno Court of Inquiry*, p. 395.

36. Donahue reinterprets the phrasing of the note from a close reading of the original artifact in the West Point Library as "Benteen Come on. Big Village. Be quick. Bring packs. W.W. Cooke & Bring packs" (*Where the Rivers Ran Red*, p. 169). I have chosen to stick with the traditional phrasing.

37. Wayne Wells, "Kanipe, Martin and Benteen," *Research Review: The Journal of the Little Big Horn Associates* 2 (Summer 1988): 10–15, 31; *Reno Court of Inquiry*, pp. 388–89, 395–97.

38. According to testimony at the court of inquiry on Reno's actions at the battle in 1879, the closest slain soldier to the ford was found two hundred to eight hundred yards east of the river. Most accounts place the body about five hundred yards from the crossing point. *Reno Court of Inquiry*, pp. 66–67, 322, 328, 417, 495, 548; Richard A. Fox, *Archaeology, History, and Custer's Last Battle: The Little Big Horn Reexamined* (Norman: University of Oklahoma Press, 1993).

39. Author discussions with Brian C. Pohanka. Pohanka never wavered in his belief that Custer's death occurred on Last Stand Hill and not at the end of Medicine Tail Coulee at the Little Big Horn River.

40. The Cheyenne soldier Wolf recounted the flight of women and children to the east side of the river: "When these women were crossing the river, and some were going up the hills, they discovered more troops coming" (Wolf, oral history, George Bird Grinnell Papers, Braun Research Library, Southwest Museum, Los Angeles, Calif.). Another Cheyenne, Tall Bull, described how "women going over east [of the river] to get on high ground to overlook Reno fight discovered Custer coming" (Camp and Thaddeus Redwater, interview with Tall Bull, 22 July 1910, in *Custer in '76*, p. 212). For an excellent summary of the location and findings at Luce and Nye-

Cartwright Ridges, *see* Bruce A. Trinque, "Elusive Ridge," *Research Review* 9 (Summer 1995): 2–8.

41. Donahue, *Where the Rivers Ran Red*, p. 186.

42. John Stands in Timber asserted "[The] Battle proper began below and west of the cemetery, [and] moved to Custer Ridge" (interview, 8 Aug. 1958, Little Bighorn Battlefield Collection, Little Bighorn National Monument). Drawing upon the oral history of Stands in Timber and other Cheyennes, Fox further develops this concept in *Archaeology, History, and Custer's Last Battle*.

43. Donahue, *Where the Rivers Ran Red*, pp. 186–90.

44. Barnard, *Photographing Custer's Battlefield*, pp. 231–33.

45. Richard G. Hardorff, *Lakota Recollections of the Custer Fight* (Spokane, Wash.: Arthur H. Clark Co., 1991), p. 147.

46. *Reno Court of Inquiry*, p. 417.

47. Camp, interview with Jacob Adams, 14 Oct. 1910, in *Custer in '76*, p. 121.

48. Stands in Timber, *Cheyenne Memories*, p. 201.

49. Graham, *Custer Myth*, p. 75.

50. For a detailed study of the Lakota approach to warfare and their likely casualties at Little Big Horn, *see* Hardorff, *Hokahey! A Good Day to Die!: The Indian Casualties of the Custer Fight* (Spokane, Wash.: Arthur H. Clark Co., 1993).

51. *Reno Court of Inquiry*, p. 236; Taunton, *Custer's Field: A Scene of Sickening Ghastly Horror* (London: The Johnson-Taunton Military Press, 1986), p. 12.

52. Edgerly, testimony, in *Reno Court of Inquiry*, pp. 453–54; Camp, interview with Edgerly, p. 58; Knipe, battle account, p. 95; Taunton, *Custer's Field*, pp. 16, 41.

53. Camp, interview with Richard E. Thompson, 14 Feb. 1911, in *Custer in '76*, p. 248; Taunton, *Custer's Field*, pp. 8, 12–13.

54. Taunton, *Custer's Field*, pp. 14–15; Hardorff, *Custer Battle Casualties, II: The Dead, the Missing, and the Few Survivors* (El Segundo, Calif.: Upton & Sons, 1999), pp. 133–34. Stands in Timber stated, "The horses of the gray horse soldiers were frightened away by Indians coming up the big ravine. . . . Indians coming from the north and from the south forced these gray horse soldiers into the Big Ravine" (Stands in Timber notes, 8 Aug. 1958, Little Bighorn Battlefield Collection).

55. Barnard, *Photographing Custer's Battlefield*, pp. 229–31; Bar-

nard, *I Go With Custer*, pp. 143–50; Donahue and Michael Moore, "Gibbon's Route to Custer Hill," *Greasy Grass* 7 (May 1991): 22–32.

56. Taunton, *Custer's Field*, p. 22. For details of the soldier remains, *see* Hardorff, *Custer Battle Casualties: Burials, Exhumations, and Reinternments* (El Segundo, Calif.: Upton & Sons, 1989), and *Custer Battle Casualties II*.

CHAPTER 6: AFTER THE LITTLE BIG HORN

1. *Bismarck Daily Tribune*, 29 June 1895. Dunn was born Christmas Day 1839 in Lawrenceburg, Indiana. In the 1850s, he lived in Indianapolis. He attended Indiana University in 1856 and fought with the Union army in the Civil War. In the early 1870s, he lived first in Brainerd, Minn., working as a druggist, before moving in mid-1872 to Edwinton, Dakota Territory, later renamed as Bismarck. Details of Dunn's life may be found in Sandy Barnard, *I Go with Custer: The Life and Death of Mark H. Kellogg* (Bismarck, N.Dak.: Bismarck Tribune Publishing, 1996), 209–10n11.

2. James E. Mueller, *Shooting Arrows and Slinging Mud: Custer, the Press, and the Little Bighorn* (Norman: University of Oklahoma Press, 2013), p. xi.

3. Numerous fine works exist on the background of the 1876 campaign. *See* Robert M. Utley, *Cavalier in Buckskin: George Armstrong Custer and the Western Military Frontier* (Norman: University of Oklahoma Press, 1988); Richard A. Fox, *Archaeology, History, and Custer's Last Battle: The Little Big Horn Reexamined* (Norman: University of Oklahoma Press, 1993); John S. Gray, *Centennial Campaign: The Sioux War of 1876* (Ft. Collins, Colo.: Old Army Press, 1976); and Jerome A. Greene, *Battles and Skirmishes of the Great Sioux War, 1876–1877* (Norman: University of Oklahoma Press, 1993).

4. Gregory J. W. Urwin, *Custer Victorious: The Civil War Battles of General George Armstrong Custer* (1983; reprint ed., Lincoln: University of Nebraska Press, 1990), p. 15.

5. Ibid., p. 9.

6. Author Loring MacKaye wrote a children's novel in 1956 that focuses on Mark Kellogg and his young friend Jon Olson, who worked as an apprentice in 1876 for the *Bismarck Tribune* (*The Great Scoop* [New York: Thomas Nelson & Sons, 1956]).

7. Utley, *Custer and the Great Controversy: The Origin and Development of a Legend* (Los Angeles: Westernlore Press, 1962), p. 29.

8. Gray, *Centennial Campaign*, p. 70.

9. *Bismarck Tribune*, 19 July 1876.

10. *Fargo (N.Dak.) Record*, Aug. 1895

11. Clement Lounsberry to Walter M. Camp, 16 Oct. 1911, Walter Mason Camp Papers, L. Tom Perry Special Collections, Harold B. Lee Library, Brigham Young University, Provo, Utah.

12. *Bismarck Tribune*, 19 July 1876. Brigadier General George Crook had a number of correspondents accompanying his Wyoming Column.

13. Material about Captain McCaskey is drawn from Dennis Farioli, Ron Nichols, and Lee Noyes, *Last Man Standing: William Spencer McCaskey* (East Longmeadow, Mass.: By the Authors, 2014), pp. 60–69.

14. Quoted in *The Custer Story: The Life and Intimate Letters of General George A. Custer and His Wife Elizabeth*, ed. Marguerite Merington (New York: Devin-Adair, 1950), p. 323.

15. Lawrence A. Frost, *General Custer's Libbie* (Seattle, Wash.: Superior Publishing, 1975), and Shirley Leckie, *Elizabeth Bacon Custer and the Making of a Myth* (Norman: University of Oklahoma Press, 1993) provide detailed accounts of Libbie Custer's reaction to her husband's death and her life in the fifty-seven years that followed.

16. Lawrence Barrett to Mollie Barrett, 26 Oct. 1876, Dayton, Ohio, Lawrence Barrett Correspondence, Harvard Theater Collection, Houghton Library, Harvard University, Cambridge, Mass. *See also* Barnard, "The Widow Custer, Consolation comes from Custer's best friend," *Greasy Grass* 17 (May 2001): 2–7.

17. Surprisingly little has been written about Barrett himself or his relationship with Custer. For more *see* Alice T. O'Neil, *The Actor and the General: The Friendship Between Lawrence Barrett and George Armstrong Custer* (Brooklyn, N.Y.: Arrow and Trooper Publishing, 1994).

18. Ibid., pp. 17–26.

19. Barrett served as the founding captain and company commander for Company B of the Twenty-eighth Massachusetts Volunteer Infantry Regiment in 1861–1862. After leading his company at the Battle of Secessionville, near Charleston, South Carolina, on 16 June 1862, he resigned his commission to return to the Boston stage. Private John Ryan, who would later serve ten years with Custer in the Seventh Cavalry, served in Company C of the same regiment.

See Barnard, *Campaigning with the Irish Brigade: Pvt. John Ryan, 28th Massachusetts* (Terre Haute, Ind.: AST Press, 2001), pp. 24–25.

20. Barrett to Barrett, 26 Oct. 1876; Barnard, "The Widow Custer."

21. *See* Frost, *General Custer's Libbie*; Leckie, *Elizabeth Bacon Custer and the Making of a Myth.*

22. Barrett to Barrett, 26 Oct. 1876; Barnard, "The Widow Custer."

23. Frost, *General Custer's Libbie*, p. 236.

24. Louise Barnett, *Touched by Fire: The Life, Death, and Mythic Afterlife of George Armstrong Custer* (New York: Henry Holt & Co., 1996), pp. 351–52.

25. *New York Herald*, 2 Sept. 1876.

26. Frost, *General Custer's Libbie*, p. 237. Frost himself was born in 1907 and died in 1990 (*New York Times*, 17 Aug. 1990).

27. *See* Barnard, *Digging Into Custer's Last Stand* (Terre Haute, Ind.: AST Press, 1998), pp. 137–47.

28. Quoted ibid., p. 138.

29. Francis B. Taunton, *Custer's Field: A Scene of Sickening Ghastly Horror* (London: Johnson-Taunton Military Press, 1989), p. 26.

30. James H. Bradley, *The March of the Montana Column: A Prelude to the Custer Disaster*, ed. Edgar I. Stewart (Norman: University of Oklahoma Press, 1961), p. 173.

31. John Ryan, "One of Custer's First Sergeants Tells Story of Reno's Part in Fight on Little Bighorn," Supplement to the *Hardin (Mont.) Tribune*, 22 June 1923, in author's possession.

32. Douglas D. Scott, Richard A. Fox, Melissa A. Connor, and Dick Harmon, *Archaeological Perspectives of the Battle of the Little Bighorn* (Norman: University of Oklahoma Press, 1989), pp. 246–47.

33. During the archaeological projects of the 1980s, and subsequently, numerous body parts of Seventh Cavalry soldiers were discovered on the battlefield. On 25 June 1986, the first group of remains the reburial party overlooked when they transferred the skeletons to the common grave in 1881 were placed in a single grave in the cemetery. The grave has been reopened on other occasions to accept additional remains. *See* Barnard, *Digging Into Custer's Last Stand*, pp. 51–52.

34. "Army may have Made a Grave Error When it Buried Custer," *Los Angeles Times*, 15 Sept. 1991.

35. Barnard, *Digging Into Custer's Last Stand*, p. 143.

36. "Army may have Made a Grave Error When it Buried Custer."

37. "Custer at Rest," *New York Herald*, 11 Oct. 1877.

38. "Funeral of Gen. Custer," *New York Times*, 11 Oct. 1877.

39. "Custer at Rest"; "Funeral of Gen. Custer."

40. "Custer at Rest"; "Funeral of Gen. Custer."

41. "Funeral of Gen. Custer."

42. Ibid.

43. "Funeral of General Custer," *Harper's Weekly*, 27 Oct. 1877.

44. Barnett, *Touched by Fire*, p. 366.

45. Frost, *General Custer's Libbie*, p. 327.

46. Quoted in James S. Robbins, *The Real Custer: From Boy General to Tragic Hero* (Washington, D.C.: Regenery Publishing, 2014), p. 417.

47. Larry Skelnar, *To Hell with Honor: Custer and the Little Bighorn* (Norman: University of Oklahoma Press, 2000), p. 37.

48. Barnett, *Touched by Fire*, p. 319.

49. T. J. Stiles, *Custer's Trials: A Life on the Frontier of a New America* (New York: Alfred A. Knopf, 2015), p. 324.

50. Greene, *Washita: The U.S. Army and the Southern Cheyennes, 1867–1869* (Norman: University of Oklahoma Press, 2004), pp. 188–93.

51. Stiles, *Custer's Trials*, p. 325.

52. James S. Brust, "Hindsight Bias & The Battle of Little Big Horn," *Research Review* 13 (Winter 1999): 22–23.

Bibliography

UNPUBLISHED MATERIALS

Archives and Historical Collections, Michigan State University
 Libraries, East Lansing, Mich.
 Edward G. Granger Journal
Archives and Manuscript Division, Oklahoma Historical Society,
 Oklahoma City
 Joseph B. Thoburn Papers
Beinecke Rare Books and Manuscripts Library, Yale University,
 New Haven, Conn.
 Barnitz Papers
Bentley Historical Library, University of Michigan, Ann Arbor
 James H. Kidd Papers
 Victor E. Comte Papers
Braun Research Library, South west Museum, Los Angeles, Calif.
 George Bird Grinnell Papers
Elwyn B. Robinson Special Collections, Chester Fritz Library,
 University of North Dakota, Grand Forks
 Frank L. Anders Papers, OGL#43-5-1
Harvard Theater Collection, Houghton Library, Harvard University,
 Cambridge, Mass.
 Lawrence Barnett Correspondence
Library of Congress, Washington, D.C.
 W. J. Ghent Papers
 Edward S. Godfrey Papers
 Philip H. Sheridan Papers
Little Bighorn Battlefield National Monument, Crow Agency, Mont.
 Elizabeth Bacon Custer Collection
 Kenneth Hammer Collection
 Little Bighorn Battlefield Collection
Monroe County Public Library, Monroe, Mich.
 George Armstrong Custer Collection
 Lawrence A. Frost Collection
National Archives and Records Administration, Washington, D.C.
 Compiled Records Showing Service of Military Units in
  Volunteer Union Organizations, microfilm, M594

Record Group 94. Records of the Adjutant General's Office
Record Group 393. Records of the U.S. Army Continental
     Command
Newberry Library, Chicago, Ill.
   Elmo Scott Watson Papers
Phoebe Apperson Hearst Memorial Library, Lead, S.Dak.
   Ralph G. Cartwright Collection
L. Tom Perry Special Collections, Harold B. Lee Library,
     Brigham Young University, Provo, Utah
   Walter Mason Camp Papers
Waldo Library, Western Michigan University, Kalamazoo
   W. H. Rockwell Letters

NEWSPAPERS

Army and Navy Journal
Associated Press
Big Horn County (Mont.) News
Billings (Mont.) Gazette
Bismarck Daily Tribune
Centerville (Ind.) Republican
Detroit Daily Advertiser
Detroit Daily Advertiser and Tribune
Detroit Free Press
Fargo (N.Dak.) Record
Great Bend (Kans.) Tribune
Great Falls (Mont.) Tribune
Hardin (Mont.) Tribune
Harpers Weekly
Indiana True Republican (Centerville, Ind.)
Indianapolis Star
Los Angeles Times
Ann Arbor Michigan Argus
Missouri Democrat
New York Herald
New York Times
Peoria (Ill.) Star
Richmond (Ind.) Weekly Palladium
Richmond (Ind.) Weekly Telegram
Wheeling (W.Va.) Register

BOOKS, JOURNAL ARTICLES, AND THESIS

Afton, Jean, David F. Halaas, Andrew E. Masich, and Richard N. Ellis. *Cheyenne Dog Soldiers: A Ledgerbook History of Coups and Combats*. Boulder: University Press of Colorado, 1997.

Armes, George A. *Ups and Downs of an Army Officer*. Washington, D.C.: n.p., 1900.

Athearn, Robert G. *William Tecumseh Sherman and the Settlement of the West*. Norman: University of Oklahoma Press, 1956.

Barnard, Sandy, ed. *An Aide to Custer: The Civil War Letters of Lt. Edward G. Granger*. Comp. Thomas E. Singelyn. Norman: University of Oklahoma Press, 2018

————, ed. *Campaigning with the Irish Brigade: Pvt. John Ryan, 28th Massachusetts*. Terre Haute, Ind.: AST Press, 2001.

————. "Custer and Elliott: Comrades in Controversy." *Fourteenth Annual Symposium Custer Battlefield Historical & Museum Association, Inc. (CBHMA) Held at Hardin, Montana, on June 23, 2000*. Hardin, Mont.: Custer Battlefield Historical & Musuem Association, 2000.

————. *Custer's First Sergeant John Ryan*. Terre Haute, Ind.: AST Press, 1996.

————. *Digging into Custer's Last Stand*. Terre Haute, Ind.: AST Press, 1998.

————. *I Go With Custer: The Life and Death of Reporter Mark Kellogg*. Bismarck, N.Dak.: Bismarck Tribune Publishing, 1996.

————. "Ken Hammer, Looking for Walter Camp." *Greasy Grass* 11 (May 1995): 20, 25–29.

————. *A Hoosier Quaker Goes to War: The Life and Death of Major Joel H. Elliott, 7th Cavalry*. Wake Forest, N.C.: AST Press, 2010.

————. "Mark Kellogg's Role during the 1876 Campaign." *1st Annual Symposium, Custer Battlefield Historical & Museum Association, Inc. (CBHMA), Held at Hardin, Montana, on June 26, 1987*. Hardin, Mont.: Custer Battlefield Historical & Museum Association, 1988.

————. *Photographing Custer's Battlefield: The Images of Kenneth F. Roahen*. Norman: University of Oklahoma Press, 2016.

————. *Shovels & Speculation: Archeology Hunts Custer*. Terre Haute, Ind.: AST Press, 1990.

————, ed. *Ten Years With Custer: A Seventh Cavalryman's Memoirs*. Terre Haute, Ind.: AST Press, 2001.

———. "The Widow Custer: Consolation Comes from Custer's Best Friend." *Greasy Grass* 17 (May 2001): 2–7.

Barnett, Louise. *Touched By Fire: The Life, Death, and Mythic Afterlife of George Armstrong Custer*. New York: Henry Holt & Co., 1996.

Berthong, Donald J. *The Cheyenne and Arapaho Ordeal*. Norman: University of Oklahoma Press, 1976.

———. *The Southern Cheyennes*. Norman: University of Oklahoma Press, 1963.

Boyes, William. "The Other Lone Tepee." *Research Review* 23 (Summer 2009): 2–9.

Brady, Cyrus Townsend. *Indian Fights and Fighters*. Lincoln, Nebr.: Bison Books, 1971.

Brill, Charles J. *Custer, Black Kettle, and the Fight on the Washita*. Norman: University of Oklahoma Press, 2002.

Brininstool, Earl A. *Troopers With Custer*. Harrisburg, Pa.: Stackpole, 1952.

Broome, Jeff. *Custer into the West*. El Segundo, Calif.: Upton & Sons, 2008.

———. "Custer's Summer Indian Campaign of 1867." *Denver Westerners Roundup* 64 (July–Aug. 2008): 3–33.

Brust, James. "Adventurous Detour to Battlefield." *Greasy Grass* 10 (May 1994): 8–12.

———. "Hindsight Bias and the Battle of the Little Bighorn." *Research Review* 13 (Winter 1999): 22–23.

———. "Lt. Oscar Long's Early Map Details Terrain, Battle Positions." *Greasy Grass* 11 (May 1995): 5–13.

———. "Norris Drew Early On-Site Map of Battle." *Greasy Grass* 10 (May 1994): 13–15.

———. "Where Was the Timber?" *11th Annual Symposium, CBHMA, Held at Hardin, Montana on June 27, 1997*. Hardin, Mont.: Custer Battlefield Historical & Museum Association, 1998.

———, Brian C. Pohanka, and Sandy Barnard. *Where Custer Fell: Photographs of the Little Bighorn Battlefield Then and Now*. Norman: University of Oklahoma Press, 2005.

Burkey, Blaine. *Custer, Come at Once!: The Fort Hays Years of George and Elizabeth Custer, 1867–1870*. Hays, Kans.: Society of Friends of Fort Hays, 1991.

Calhoun, James. *With Custer in '74: James Calhoun's Diary of the Black Hills Expedition*. Provo, Utah: Brigham Young University Press, 1979.

Carriker, Robert C. *Fort Supply, Indian Territory*. Norman: University of Oklahoma Press, 1970.

Carrington, Henry B. *The Indian Question*. New York: Sol Lewis, 1973.

Carroll, John, ed. *The Benteen-Goldin Letters on Custer and His Last Battle*. New York: Liveright, 1974.

———. *Custer in Texas: An Interrupted Narrative*. New York: Sol Lewis/Liveright, 1975.

———. *General Custer and the Battle of the Washita: The Federal View*. Bryan, Tex.: Guidon Press, 1974.

———. "The Little Big Horn Medals of Honor." *Research Review* 4 (Jan. 1990): 20–32.

———. "Major Wickcliffe Cooper, 7th U. S. Cavalry—Was It Murder or Suicide?" *Research Review* 2 (Dec. 1986): 6–17.

——— and Byron Price. *Roll Call On The Little Big Horn, 28 June 1876*. Fort Collins, Colo: The Old Army Press, 1974.

Chandler, Melbourne C. *Of Garryowen in Glory: The History of the 7th Cavalry*. Annandale, Va.: Turnpike Press, 1960.

Chernow, Ron. *Grant*. New York: Penguin Press, 2017.

Clark, George M. *Scalp Dance: The Edgerly Papers on the Battle of the Little Big Horn*. Oswego, N.Y.: Heritage Press, 1985.

Coffman, Edward M. *The Old Army: A Portrait of the American Army in Peacetime, 1784–1898*. New York: Oxford University Press, 1986.

Cogley, Thomas S. *History of the 7th Indiana Cavalry*. Dayton, Ohio: Morningside, 1991.

Cooper, David M. *Obituary Discourse on Occasion of the Death of Noah Henry Ferry, Major of the 5th Michigan Cavalry, Killed at Gettysburg, July 3, 1863*. New York: John F. Trow, 1863.

Cowdrey, Mike. "Crows who Scouted for Custer." *Greasy Grass* 14 (May 1998): 39–44.

Cozzens, Peter. *Eyewitnesses to the Indian Wars, 1865–1890: Conquering the Southern Plains*. Mechanicsburg, Pa.: Stackpole, 2003.

Crary, Catherine S. *Dear Belle: Letters From a Cadet and Officer to his Sweetheart, 1858–1865*. Middletown, Conn.: Wesleyan University Press, 1965.

Curtis, Edward. *The North American Indian: Being a Series of Volumes Picturing and Describing The Indians of the United States and Alaska*. Cambridge, Mass.: Harvard University Press, 1908.

Custer, Elizabeth B. "General Custer and the Indian Chiefs." *Outlook Magazine*. July 1927.

———. *Tenting on the Plains; Or General Custer in Kansas and Texas*. New York: Charles L. Webster, 1887.

Custer, George Armstrong. *My Life on the Plains*. 1874; reprint ed., Lincoln, Nebr.: Bison Books, 1972.

———. "War Memoirs." *Galaxy* 21 (June 1876): 810–20.

Custer National Cemetery. Little Bighorn Battlefield National Monument, Mont.: Southwest Parks & Monuments Association, 1999.

Darling, Roger. *Benteen's Scout to the Left: The Route from the Divide to the Morass, June 25, 1876*. El Segundo, Calif.: Upton & Sons, 1987.

Despain, S. Matthew. "Captain Albert Barnitz and the Battle of the Washita, New Documents, New Insights." *Journal of the Indian Wars* 1 (1999): 134–44.

Donahue, Michael and Michael Moore. "Gibbon's Route to Custer Hill." *Greasy Grass* 7 (May 1991): 22–32.

Donahue, Michael N. *Drawing Battle Lines: The Map Testimony of Custer's Last Fight*. El Segundo, Calif.: Upton & Sons, 2008.

———. "Knipe's Recollections Help Camp Reconstruct Custer's Final Hours." *Greasy Grass* 14 (May 1998): 2–17.

———. "Revisiting Col. Gibbon's Route." *Greasy Grass* 19 (May 2003): 12–20.

———. *Where the Rivers Ran Red: The Indian Fights of George Armstrong Custer*. Montrose, Colo.: San Juan Publishing, 2018.

Donovan, James. *A Terrible Glory: Custer and the Little Bighorn—the Last Great Battle of the West*. New York: Little, Brown, 2008.

Dustin, Fred. *The Custer Tragedy Events leading Up to And Following the Little Big Horn Campaign of 1876*. 1939; reprint ed., El Segundo, Calif.: Upton & Sons, 2011.

Eicher, John and David J. Eicher. *Civil War High Commands*. Stanford, Calif.: Stanford University Press, 2001.

Ediger, Theodore A. and Vinnie Hoffman. "Some Reminiscences

of the Battle of Washita." *Chronicles of Oklahoma* 33 (Summer 1935): 137–41.

Ellison, Douglas. *Sole Survivor*. Aberdeen, S.Dak.: North Plains Press, 1983.

Epple, Jess C. *Custer's Battle of the Washita and the History of the Plains Indian Tribes*. Jericho, N.Y.: Exposition Press, 1970.

Farioli, Dennis, Ronald Nichols, and Lee Noyes. *Last Man Standing: William Spencer McCaskey*. East Longmeadow, Mass.: n.p., 2014.

Foley, James R. "Walter Camp & Ben Clark." *Research Review* 9 (Jan. 1996): 17–28.

Foner, Eric. *Reconstruction: America's Unfinished Revolution, 1863–1877*. New York: Harper & Row, 1988.

Fox, Richard. *Archaeology, History, and Custer's Last Battle: The Little Big Horn Reexamined*. Norman: University of Oklahoma Press, 1993.

Frost, Lawrence A., *The Court-Martial of General George Armstrong Custer*. Norman: University of Oklahoma Press, 1968.

———. *The Custer Album: A Pictorial Biography of General George A. Custer*. New York: Bonanza Books, 1984.

———. *Custer's 7th Cavalry and the Campaign of 1873*. El Segundo, Calif.: Upton & Sons, 1986.

———. *General Custer's Libbie*. Seattle, Wash.: Superior Publishing Co., 1975.

Galvin, Kevin E., ed. *Confrontation along the Washita: A Collection of Essays*. London: Western Publications Limited, 2003.

Gerber, Max E. "The Custer Expedition of 1874: A New Look." *North Dakota History* 40 (Winter 1973): 5–26.

Godfrey, Edward S. "Custer's Last Battle." *Century Monthly Illustrated Magazine* 43 (Jan. 1892): 358–84.

———. "The Medicine Lodge Treaty, Sixty Years Ago." *Winners of the West* 6 (Mar. 1929): 8.

———. "Some Reminiscences, Including an Account of General Sully's Expedition against the Southern Plains Indians, 1868." *Cavalry Journal* 36 (July 1927): 417–25.

———. "The Washita Campaign," *Winners of the West* 6 (Apr.–July 1929).

Gorman, Paul R. "J. E. B. Stuart and Gettysburg." *Gettysburg Magazine* 1 (July 1989): 86–92.

Grady, Timothy P. and Melissa Walker, eds. *Recovering the Piedmont Past: Unexplored Moments in Nineteenth-Century Upcountry South Carolina History*. Columbia: University of South Carolina Press, 2013.

Grafe, Ernest and Paul Horsted. *Exploring with Custer: The 1874 Black Hills Expedition*. Custer, S.Dak.: Golden Valley Press, 2002.

Graham, William A. *The Custer Myth: A Source Book of Custeriana*. New York: Bonanza Books, 1953.

———. *Story of the Little Big Horn: Custer's Last Fight*. New York: Bonanza Books, 1926.

Gray, John. *Centennial Campaign: The Sioux War of 1876*. Norman: University of Oklahoma Press, 1988.

———. *Custer's Last Campaign: Mitch Boyer and the Little Bighorn Reconstructed*. Lincoln: University of Nebraska Press, 1991.

Greene, Jerome A. *Battles and Skirmishes of the Great Sioux War, 1876–1877*. Norman: University of Oklahoma Press, 1993.

———. *Evidence and the Custer Enigma: A Reconstruction of Indian-Military History*. Golden, Colo.: Outdoor Books, 1986.

———. *Stricken Field: The Little Bighorn since 1876*. Norman: University of Oklahoma Press, 2008.

———. *Washita: The U.S. Army and the Southern Cheyennes, 1867–1869*. Norman: University of Oklahoma Press, 2004.

Hammer, Kenneth, ed. *Custer in '76: Walter Camp's Notes on the Custer Fight*. Provo, Utah: Brigham Young University Press, 1976.

——— and Ronald Nichols, eds. *Men With Custer: Biographies of the 7th Cavalry*. Hardin, Mont.: Custer Battlefield Historical & Museum Association, 1995.

Hardorff, Richard G., ed. *Camp, Custer and the Little Bighorn*. El Segundo, Calif.: Upton & Sons, 1997.

———. *Cheyenne Memories of the Custer Fight*. Spokane, Wash.: Arthur H. Clark Co., 1995.

———. *The Custer Battle Casualties: Burials, Exhumations, and Reinterments*. El Segundo, Calif.: Upton & Sons, 1989.

———. *The Custer Battle Casualties, II: The Dead, the Missing, and a Few Survivors*. El Segundo, Calif.: Upton & Sons, 1999.

———. *Hokahey! A Good Day to Die!: The Indian Casualties of the Custer Fight*. Spokane, Wash.: Arthur H. Clark Co., 1993.

———. *Lakota Recollections of the Custer Fight*. Spokane, Wash.: Arthur H. Clark Co., 1991.

———, ed. *On The Little Bighorn With Walter Camp: A Collection of W.M. Camp's Letters, Notes and Opinions on Custer's Last Fight*. El Segundo, Calif.: Upton & Sons, 2002.

———. *Walter M. Camp's Little Bighorn Rosters*. Spokane, Wash.: Arthur H. Clark Co., 2002.

———. *Washita Memories: Eyewitness Views of Custer's Attack on Black Kettle's Village*. Norman: University of Oklahoma Press, 2005.

Harrison, Peter. *The Eyes of the Sleepers: Cheyenne Accounts of the Washita Attack*. London: English Westerners Society, 1998.

———. *Monahsetah*. London: English Westerners Society, 2015.

Hatch, Thom. *Black Kettle: The Cheyenne Chief Who Sought Peace but Found War*. Hoboken, N.J.: Wiley & Sons, 2004.

Hedegaard, Michael L. "Colonel Joseph J. Reynolds and the Saint Patrick's Day Celebration on Powder River: Battle of Powder River (Montana, 17 March 1876)." Master's thesis, U.S. Army Command and General Staff College, 2001.

Hedren, Paul L. *Great Sioux War Orders of Battle: How the United States Waged War on the Northern Plains, 1876–1877*. Norman, Okla.: Arthur H. Clark Co., 2011.

———. "Holy Ground, The United States Army Embraces Custer's Battlefield." in *Legacy: New Perspectives on the Battle of Little Bighorn*. Ed. Charles E. Rankin, pp. 189–206. Helena: Montana Historical Society Press, 1996.

———. *Powder River: Disastrous Opening of the Great Sioux War*. Norman: University of Oklahoma Press, 2016.

———. *With Crook in the Black Hills: Stanley J. Morrow's 1876 Photographic Legacy*. Boulder, Colo.: Pruett Publishing, 1985.

Heski, Thomas. *The Little Shadow Catcher: D.F. Barry, Celebrated Photographer of Famous Indians*. Seattle, Wash.: Superior Publishing, 1978.

Hoig, Stan. *The Battle of the Washita*. Lincoln: University of Nebraska Press, 1979.

———. *The Peace Chiefs of the Cheyennes*. Norman: University of Oklahoma Press, 1980.

———. *The Sand Creek Massacre*. Norman: University of Oklahoma Press, 1961.

————. *Tribal Wars of the Southern Plains*. Norman: University of Oklahoma Press, 1993.

Howe, Henry. "A Talk with John Giles of Scio." *Historical Collections of Ohio*. Vol. 1. Columbus, Ohio: Henry Howe & Son, 1891.

Hutchins, James, ed. *The Papers of Edward S. Curtis Relating to Custer's Last Battle*. El Segundo, Calif.: Upton & Sons, 2000.

Hutton, Paul Andrew, ed. *The Custer Reader*. Lincoln: University of Nebraska Press, 1992.

————. *Phil Sheridan and His Army*. Lincoln: University of Nebraska Press, 1985.

Isham, Asa B. *Seventh Michigan Cavalry of Custer's Wolverine Brigade*. Huntington, W.Va.: Blue Acorn Press, 2000.

Jackson, Donald. *Custer's Gold: The United States Cavalry Expedition of 1874*. New Haven, Conn.: Yale University Press, 1966.

Johnson, Randy and Nancy Allen. *A Dispatch to Custer: The Tragedy of Lieutenant Kidder*. Missoula, Mont.: Mountain Press Publishing, 1999.

Jones, Douglas C. *The Treaty of Medicine Lodge: The Story of the Great Treaty Council As Told by Eyewitnesses*. Norman: University of Oklahoma Press, 1966.

Jones, Virgil Carrington. *Ranger Mosby*. Chapel Hill: University of North Carolina Press, 1944.

Justus, Judith P. "The Saga of Clara H. Blinn at the Battle of the Washita." *Research Review* 14 (Winter 2000): 11–20.

Kidd, James H., *A Cavalryman with Custer: Custer's Michigan Cavalry Brigade in the Civil War*. New York: Bantam Books, 1991.

————. *Personal Recollections of a Cavalryman with Custer's Michigan Cavalry Brigade in the Civil War*. Grand Rapids, Mich.: The Black Letter Press, 1969.

Koster, John. *Custer Survivor: The End of a Myth, the Beginning of a Legend*. Palisades, N.Y.: History Publishing Co., 2010.

Kraft, Louis. *Custer and the Cheyenne*. El Segundo, Calif.: Upton & Sons, 1995.

Kuhlman, Charles. *Legend Into History*. Fort Collins, Colo.: The Old Army Press, 1977.

Lazarus, Edward. *Black Hills, White Justice: The Sioux Nation Versus the United States, 1775 to the Present*. New York: HarperCollins, 1991.

Leckie, Shirley A. *Elizabeth Bacon Custer and the Making of a Myth.*
Norman: University of Oklahoma Press, 1993.

Leckie, William H. *The Military Conquest of the Southern Plains.*
Norman: University of Oklahoma Press, 1963.

Lee, William O., comp. *Personal and Historical Sketches and Facial
History of and by Members of the Seventh Regiment Michigan
Volunteer Cavalry 1862–1865.* 1902; reprint ed., London:
Forgotten Books, 2015.

Lees, William B. "Archaeological Evidence: The Attack on Black
Kettle's Village on the Washita River." *Journal of the Indian Wars*
1 (Spring 1999): 33–42.

Libby, Orin Grant. *Arikara Narrative of the Campaign Against the
Hostile Dakotas June, 1876.* New York: Sol Lewis, 1973.

Liddic, Bruce and Paul Harbaugh. *Camp on Custer: Transcending the
Custer Myth.* Spokane, Wash.: Arthur H. Clark Co., 1995.

Liddic, Bruce. *Vanishing Victory: Custer's Final March.* El Segundo,
Calif.: Upton & Sons, 2004.

Longacre, Edward G. *Custer and His Wolverines: The Michigan
Cavalry Brigade, 1861–1865.* Conshohocken, Pa.: Combined
Publishing, 1997.

Lottinville, Savoie, ed. *Life of George Bent Written from His Letters.*
Norman: University of Oklahoma Press, 1968.

Lubetkin, M. John, ed. *Custer and the 1873 Yellowstone Survey:
A Documentary History.* Norman, Okla.: Arthur H. Clark Co., 2013.
———. *Jay Cooke's Gamble: The Northern Pacific Railroad, the Sioux,
and the Panic of 1873.* Norman: University of Oklahoma Press,
2006.

Luce, Moses A. "Custer's First Battle by One Who Took Part in It as
a Member of the Fourth Michigan." *Overland Monthly and Out
West Magazine* 31 (Jan.–June 1898): 280–81.

MacKaye, Loring. *The Great Scoop.* New York: Thomas Nelson &
Sons, 1956.

Magnussen, Daniel O., ed. *Peter Thompson's Narrative of the Little
Bighorn Campaign.* Glendale, Calif.: Arthur H. Clark Co., 1974.

Marquis, Thomas. *Wooden Leg: A Warrior Who Fought Custer.*
Lincoln: University of Nebraska Press, 1931.

Martinez, J. Michael. *Carpetbaggers, Cavalry, and the Ku Klux Klan:
Exposing the Invisible Empire During Reconstruction.* Lanham,
Md.: Rowman & Littlefield, 2007.

McClellan, George B. *McClellan's Own Story: The War for the Union*. New York: Charles L. Webster, 1887.

Meketa, Ray and Thomas E. Bookwalter. *The Search for the Lone Tepee*. n.p.: Little Horn Press, 1983.

Merington, Marguerite, ed. *The Custer Story: The Life and Intimate Letters of General Custer and His Wife Elizabeth*. New York: Devin-Adair, 1950.

Michno, Gregory. *Lakota Noon*. Missoula, Mont.: Mountain Press Publishing, 1997.

———. *The Mystery of E Troop: Custer's Gray Horse Company at the Little Bighorn*. Missoula, Mont.: Mountain Press Publishing, 1994.

Millbrook, Minnie Dubbs. "The West Breaks in General Custer." *Kansas Historical Quarterly* 36 (Summer 1970): 113–48.

Mills, Charles K. *Harvest of Barren Regrets: The Army Career of Frederick William Benteen, 1834–1898*. Glendale, Calif.: Arthur H. Clark Co., 1985.

Monaghan, Jay. *Custer: The Life of General George Armstrong Custer*. Boston: Little, Brown, 1959.

Monnett, John H. *The Battle of Beecher Island and the Indian War of 1867–1869*. Niwot: University Press of Colorado, 1992.

Mort, Terry. *Thieves Road: The Black Hills Betrayal and Custer's Path to Little Bighorn*. Amherst, New York: Prometheus Books, 2015.

Mueller, James E. *Shooting Arrow & Slinging Mud: Custer, the Press, and the Little Bighorn*. Norman: University of Oklahoma Press, 2013.

Neihardt, John G. *Black Elk Speaks*. Lincoln: University of Nebraska Press, 1995.

Nichols, Ronald. "CBHMA marks its 50th year." *Greasy Grass* 19 (May 2003): 3.

———. *In Custer's Shadow: Major Marcus Reno*. Fort Collins, Colo.: The Old Army Press, 1999.

———, ed. *Reno Court of Inquiry*. Crow Agency, Mont.: Custer Battlefield Historical & Museum Association, 1992.

Nye, Wilbur S. *Carbine and Lance: The Story of Old Fort Sill*. Norman: University of Oklahoma Press, 1969.

O'Neil, Alice T. *The Actor and the General: The Friendship Between Lawrence Barrett and George Armstrong Custer*. Brooklyn, N.Y.: Arrow and Trooper Publishing, 1994.

O'Neill, Robert F. *Chasing Jeb Stuart and John Mosby: The Union Cavalry in Northern Virginia from Second Manassas to Gettysburg.* Jefferson, N.C.: McFarland, 2012.

Reynolds, Arlene. *The Civil War Memories of Elizabeth Bacon Custer.* Austin: University of Texas Press, 1994.

Rhea, Gordon C. *The Battles for Spotsylvania Court House and the Road to Yellow Tavern, May 7–12, 1864.* Baton Rouge: Louisiana State University Press, 1997.

Rickey, Don, Jr. *Forty Miles a Day on Beans and Hay: The Enlisted Soldier Fighting the Indian Wars.* 1963; reprint ed., Norman: University of Oklahoma Press, 2013.

———. *History of Custer Battlefield.* Billings, Mont.: Custer Battlefield Historical & Museum Association, 1967.

Robbins, James S. *The Real Custer: From Boy General to Tragic Hero.* Washington, D.C.: Regenery Publishing, 2014.

Robertson, John, comp. *Michigan in the War.* Lansing, Mich.: W. S. George & Co., 1880.

Ronsheim, Milton. *The Life of General Custer.* Monroe, Mich.: Monroe County Public Library System, 1978.

Rush, Frank. "What Indian Tongues Could Tell: The Red Man's Story of the Conquest of the Western Plains." *Wilds and Waters* 3 (Dec. 1930–Jan. 1931): 11–13, 27, 34.

Russell, Don. *Custer's Last.* Fort Worth, Tex.: Amon Carter Museum of Western Art, 1968.

Safford, Charles H. *I Rode With Custer: The Civil War Diary of Charles H. Safford, Brevet Major, 5th Michigan Cavalry.* Ed. Paul Davis. Detroit, Mich.: Ashton Z. Publishing, 2015.

Scott, Douglas D. and Peter Bleed. *A Good Walk Around the Boundary: Archaeological Inventory of the Dyck and Other Properties Adjacent to Little Bighorn Battlefield National Monument.* Lincoln: Nebraska Association of Professional Archaeologists and Nebraska State Historical Society, 1997.

——— and Richard A. Fox. *Archaeological Insights into the Custer Battle: An Assessment of the 1984 Field Season.* Norman: University of Oklahoma Press, 1987.

———, Richard A. Fox, Melissa A. Connor, and Dick Harmon. *Archaeological Perspectives on the Battle of the Little Bighorn.* Norman: University of Oklahoma Press, 1989.

——— and P. Willey. *Osteological Analysis of Human Skeletons*

Excavated from the Custer National Cemetery. Technical Report
No. 50. Lincoln, Nebr.: Midwest Archaeological Center, 1997.

————, P. Willey, and Melissa Connor. *They Died With Custer:
Soldiers' Bones from the Battle of the Little Big Horn. Norman*:
University of Oklahoma Press, 1998.

————. *Uncovering History: Archaeological Investigations at the Little
Bighorn*. Norman: University of Oklahoma Press, 2013.

Self, Zenobia. "Court-Martial of J. J. Reynolds." *Military Affairs* 37
(Apr. 1973): 52–56.

Sheridan, Philip H. *Personal Memoirs of P. H. Sheridan*. 2 vols. New
York: Charles L. Webster & Co., 1888.

Shevchuk, Paul M. "The Battle of Hunterstown, Pennsylvania, July
2, 1863." *Gettysburg Magazine* 1 (July 1989): 93–104.

Shoemaker, John O. *The Custer Court-Martial*. Fort Leavenworth,
Kans.: Fort Leavenworth Historical Society, 1971.

Sills, Joe, Jr. "The Crow Scouts: Their Contribution in
Understanding the Little Big Horn Battle." *5th Annual
Symposium CBHMA, Held at Hardin, Montana, June 21, 1991*.
Hardin, Mont.: Custer Battlefield Historical & Museum
Association, 1992.

————. "Weir Point Perspective." *7th Annual Symposium, CBHMA,
Held at Hardin, Montana, on June 25, 1993*. Hardin, Mont.:
Custer Battlefield Historical & Museum Association, 1994.

————. "Were There Two Last Stands?" *2nd Annual Symposium,
CBHMA, Held at Hardin, Montana, June 24, 1988*. Hardin, Mont.:
Custer Battlefield Historical & Museum Association, 1989.

Skelnar, Larry. *To Hell with Honor: Custer and the Little Bighorn*.
Norman: University of Oklahoma Press, 2000.

Spotts, David L. *Campaigning with Custer and the Nineteeth Kansas
Volunteer Cavalry on the Washita Campaign, 1868–1869*. Ed.
Earl A. Brininstool. Los Angeles: Wetzel, 1928.

Slotkin, Richard. *The Fatal Environment: The Myth of the Frontier in
the Age of Industrialization, 1800–1890*. Norman: University of
Oklahoma Press, 1994.

Stands In Timber, John and Margot Liberty. *Cheyenne Memories*.
Lincoln: University of Nebraska Press, 1967.

Starr, Stephen Z. *The Union Cavalry in the Civil War: The War in the
East From Gettysburg to Appomattox 1863-1865*. Vol. 2. Baton
Rouge: Louisiana State University Press, 1981.

Stewart, Edgar I. *Custer's Luck*. Norman: University of Oklahoma Press, 1955.

Stiles, T. J. *Custer's Trials: A Life on the Frontier of a New America*. New York: Alfred A. Knopf, 2015.

Stoker, Donald. *The Grand Design: Strategy and the U.S. Civil War*. New York: Oxford University Press, 2010.

Sully, Langdon. *No Tears for the General: The Life of Alfred Sully, 1821–1879*. Palo Alto, Calif.: American West Publishing, 1974.

Taunton, Francis. *Custer's Field: A Scene of Sickening Ghastly Horror*. London: The Johnson-Taunton Military Press, 1986.

———. "The Enigma of Weir Point." *No Pride in the Little Big Horn*. Ed. Francis Taunton. London: The English Westerners' Society, 1987.

Trinque, Bruce A. "Elusive Ridge." *Research Review* 9 (Summer 1995): 2–8.

Trout, Robert J., ed. *Memoirs of the Stuart Horse Artillery Battalion*. Vol. 2. Knoxville: University of Tennessee Press, 2010.

Tuttle, Jud. "Who Buried Lieutenant Hodgson?" *4th Annual Symposium CBHMA, Held at Hardin, Montana on June 22, 1990*. Hardin, Mont.: Custer Battlefield Historical & Museum Association, 1991.

Ullery, Jacob G., comp. *Men of Vermont: An Illustrated Biographical History of Vermonters and Sons of Vermont*. Brattleboro, Vt.: Transcript Publishing, 1894.

Upton, Richard, comp. and ed. *Fort Custer on the Big Horn, 1877–1898*. Glendale, Calif.: Arthur H. Clark, 1973.

———. "The Custer Adventure." *The Brian C. Pohanka 26th Annual Symposium Custer Battlefield Historical & Museum Association held at Hardin, Montana, on June 22, 2012*. Hardin, Mont.: Custer Battlefield Historical & Museum Association, 2013.

Urwin, Gregory J. W. *Custer Victorious: The Civil War Battles of General George Armstrong Custer*. 1983; reprint ed., Lincoln: University of Nebraska Press, 1990.

U.S. Department of War. *The War of the Rebellion: A Compilation of the Official Records of the Union and Confederate Armies*. 70 vols. Washington, D.C.: Government Printing Office, 1880–1901.

Utley, Robert M. *Custer and the Great Controversy: The Origin and Development of a Legend*. Los Angeles: Westernlore Press, 1962.

————. *Frontier Regulars: The United States Army and the Indian, 1866–1891*. New York: Macmillan, 1973.

————, ed. *Life in Custer's Cavalry: Diaries and Letters of Albert and Jennie Barnitz, 1867–1868*. Lincoln: University of Nebraska Press, 1987.

————. *Cavalier in Buckskin: George Armstrong Custer and the Western Military Frontier*. Norman: University of Oklahoma Press, 1988.

Van de Water, Frederic. *Glory-Hunter: A Life of General Custer*. Lincoln: University of Nebraska Press, 1988.

Venter, Bruce M. *Kill Jeff Davis: The Union Raid on Richmond, 1864*. Norman: University of Oklahoma Press, 2016.

Viola, Herman J. *Little Bighorn Remembered: The Untold Story of Custer's Last Stand*. New York: Times Books, 1999.

Wallace, Charles B. *Custer's Ohio Boyhood: A Brief Account of the Early Life of Major General George Armstrong Custer*. Cadiz, Ohio: Harrison County Historical Society, 1993.

Warner, Ezra J. *Generals in Blue: Lives of the Union Commanders*. Baton Rouge: Louisiana State University Press, 1989.

————. *Generals in Gray: Lives of the Confederate Commanders*. Baton Rouge: Louisiana State University Press, 1959.

Wathen, R. Norvelle. *The Custer Battlefield: An Aerial Perspective*. Louisville, Ky.: R. N. Wathen, 1976.

Watson, Elmo Scott and Don Russell, "The Battle of the Washita, or Custer's Massacre?" *The Westerners Brand Books* 5 (Nov. 1948): 49–51.

Watson, Elmo, "Photographing the Frontier." *The Westerner's Brand Book* 4 (Jan. 1948): 61–62, 65–67.

————. "Theodore R. Davis, Indian War Correspondent." *The Westerner's Brand Book* 1 (Jan. 1945): 97–130.

————. "Way Out West, The Story of Stanley J. Morrow, a Pioneer Photographer in Every Sense of the Word." *Coronet*, 5 (Apr. 1939).

Weibert, Henry. *Sixty-six Years in Custer's Shadow*. Billings, Mont.: Bannack Publishing, 1985.

Welker, David A. *Tempest at Ox Hill: The Battle of Chantilly*. Cambridge, Mass.: Da Capo Press, 2002.

Wells, Wayne. "Custer's Arrival Time at the River." *1st Annual Symposium CBHMA, Held at Hardin, Montana, June 26, 1987*.

Hardin, Mont.: Custer Battlefield Historical & Museum
Association, 1988.

———. "The Fight on Calhoun Hill." *2nd Annual Symposium,
CBHMA, Held at Hardin, Montana, June 24, 1988*. Hardin, Mont.:
Custer Battlefield Historical & Museum Association, 1989.

———. "Kanipe, Martin and Benteen." *Research Review: The
Journal of the Little Big Horn Associates* 2 (Summer 1988): 10–15,
31.

———. "Little Big Horn Notes: Stanley Vestal's Indian Insights."
Greasy Grass 5 (May 1989): 9–19.

Wengert, James W. and E. Elden Davis, eds. *That Fatal Day: Eight
More With Custer*. Howell, Mich.: Powder River Press, 1992.

Wert, Jeffry D. *Custer: The Controversial Life of George Armstrong
Custer*. New York: Simon & Schuster, 1996.

———. *Mosby's Rangers*. New York: Simon & Schuster, 1990.

West, Jerry L. *The Reconstruction Ku Klux Klan in York County, South
Carolina, 1865–1877*. Jefferson, N.C.: McFarland, 2002.

White, Lonnie J. "General Sully's Expedition of the North
Canadian, 1868." *Journal of the West* 11 (Jan. 1972): 75–98.

Whittaker, Frederick. *A Complete Life of General George A. Custer*.
2 vols. 1876; reprint ed., Lincoln: University of Nebraska Press,
1993.

Wiebert, Henry and Don Wiebert. *Sixty-six Years in Custer's
Shadow*. Billings, Mont.: Falcon Press, 1985.

Wittenberg, Eric. *Glory Enough for All: Sheridan's Second Raid and
the Battle of Trevilian Station*. Washington, D.C.: Brassey's,
2000.

———, ed. *One of Custer's Wolverines: The Civil War Letters of
Brevet Brigadier General James H. Kidd, 6th Michigan Cavalry*.
Kent, Ohio: Kent State University Press, 2000.

———. *Under Custer's Command: The Civil War Journal of James
Henry Avery*. Washington, D.C.: Brassey's, 2000.

WEBSITES
Ancestry.com
Findagrave.com

Index

New York Life Insurance Co., 137

New York Times, 147

Ninth Virginia Cavalry Regiment, 25

"Nomad" (pseudonym), 82

Noonan, John, 96

Northern Cheyenne. *See* Cheyenne Indians

Northern Pacific Railroad, 83–84, 89–90, 105, 130. *See also* Railroads

Oklahoma, xiv, 51, 55, 60. *See also* Battle of the Washita

Olson, Jon, 176n6

One Stab (Hunkpapa Lakota), 96, 98

126th Ohio Volunteer Infantry Regiment, 157n15

Paiute Indians, 104

Panic of 1873, 90, 103

Parker, George, 147

Patchan, Scott C., 35–36

Pawnee Killer (Oglala Lakota), 46

Pelham, John, 10

Peninsula Campaign, 13. *See also* Army of Northern Virginia (Confederate); Army of the Potomac (U.S.); Battle of New Bridge; Battle of Seven Pines; Civil War

Pennington, Alexander, 24

Pennington's Battery, 26

Philadelphia, Penn., xi

Pickard, Edwin, 122

Pickett's Charge, 23, 27. *See also* Battle of Gettysburg

Pleasonton, Alfred, 16, 18–19, 23, 28, 31. *See also* Battle of Gettysburg; Custer, George Armstrong, military career; Grant, Ulysses S.; Meade, George Gordon

Pohanka, Brian C., xi, 118, 123, 172n21, 174n39

Porter, Henry R., 121

Poughkeepsie (N.Y.) Military Institute, 147

Powder River country, 92, 104–05, 108–10, 114–15

Race/racism, xvii, xix, 63, 133

Railroads, xvi, 41, 43, 83, 89–90, 131. *See also* Northern Pacific Railroad

Ramseur, Stephen Dodson, 10

Reconstruction, 40, 63–64, 131. *See also* Seventh U.S. Cavalry Regiment

Red Cloud (Oglala chief), 42, 99

Red Cloud's War, 44

Reed, Arthur, 128

Reed, David, 4, 157n17

Reed, Lydia Ann Kirkpatrick, 1, 4–5

Reno, Marcus A., 57, 84, 89, 106, 110–11, 114, 116–21, 123, 126–29, 139–40, 172n21, 172n23, 174n38. *See also* Battle of the Little Big Horn

Reno Creek, 114, 116, 122. *See also* Battle of the Little Big Horn

Reynolds, Charley, 96